This book is for you if...

If you are a CEO, managing director or business owner who has employees, this book is for you. If you want to create a high performing business culture that allows employees to be more productive and engaged through improved mindset and wellbeing, and that encourages employees to develop into leaders to drive your business forward, this book can help.

This book is for you if you want your business and your employees to achieve:

- Less sickness absence

- Reduced 'presenteeism' and improved productivity

- Increased profitability

- Improved employee engagement

- Happier customers

- Improved employee retention

- An organisation that attracts new talent

- Improved work/life balance

- Less stress

- A positive attitude

- Personal and professional goals

- Energy in abundance

- A competitive advantage

About the Author

Adam Strong is a corporate productivity authority, entrepreneur, athlete, coach, speaker and trainer. Adam has been featured on the BBC, in The Guardian and in People Management, HR Grapevine and Global Woman magazines. He creates and implements bespoke productivity enhancement programmes for businesses that want to see increased profitability, more engaged employees and a healthier workforce.

He is the creator of a revolutionary 5-pillar programme designed specifically to get companies up to a 300% return on investment on their high salaried executives both in the short term by reducing absenteeism and presenteeism, and in the long term by improving retention. His clients know him for using his experience as a former elite athlete to create high performing work cultures. Adam's clients can expect their businesses to be more productive and profitable, and to fulfill employees' potential both in their professional and personal lives.

Adam loves helping people, it's in his DNA, and his mission is to solve the productivity crisis that affects not just businesses but entire economies.

Adam lives in Windsor, Berkshire. His passions include travel, scuba diving, sport, and anything to do with the sea plus - most important of all - spending time with his children.

What people are saying about Adam

"This book is great - easy to read and digest and very pragmatic. Reading it is like having a friend hold up a mirror to ask the question, what really matters? why it matters? And to give a proverbial kick up the bottom to make it matter! It isn't preachy or overly theoretical but supportive and motivational and well suited to anyone whether in business or not - it certainly gets you thinking and wanting to take action."

Moorna Dason-Barber, EMEA HR Director,

British Standards Institution

"Adam's approach to mastering your own destiny resonates with my own experience - the work is spot on when it comes to a perfect work, life and health balance."

Sean Wall, Executive Vice- President,

Network Operations and Aviation for DHL

"A practical guide to getting fit with fantastic tips... I highly recommend this book!"

Darshana Ubl, Founder of Verve Rally and Former CEO of Entrevo

"This book is full of straightforward yet empowering tools to motivate you to make small changes to achieve a healthy balanced life in all your spheres of influence. There's nothing to lose and everything to gain by embarking this journey."

Arpita Dutt, Brahams, Dutt, Badrick and French,

Top Tier in Employment Law

"I've trained with Adam for a number of years. His expertise and encouragement have been invaluable, not just in helping me improve and maintain my physical health but also in helping guide me with my nutrition and stress-management. Adam is also great fun to work with so that even when the going gets tough and I'm being pushed to the next level, there's always time for a joke and

plenty of laughter - vital components of well-being and feeling good!"

David Gibbons (Suffolk, UK), Retired Public Relations Executive

"Adam puts the fun back into training. His sessions give variety and a full body workout, without just focusing on the main muscles. His vast and varied knowledge of nutrition and the dynamics of how the human body works helps him tailor the right sessions so you can meet your goals in the right way."

Prakash Radhakrishnan (Berkshire, UK), Business Owner

"My posture is poor and I suffer with painful hips and back because of how I stand. I have been training with Adam for about 12 months; and my posture has improved – as well as my stamina and general fitness.

"His sports science degree, training and background in athletics all contribute to the fact that he really does understand the body, and he uses different techniques and varies the exercises we do each time – testing and changing until we find the one that works.

"I would not hesitate to recommend him. His knowledge and experience mean that you get a totally different type of personal training than you would at a gym. It is tailored to you, and Adam spends the first session assessing your needs before starting a programme that is just right for you."

Louise Walker (Buckinghamshire, UK), Marketing Specialist

"I have been working with Adam as my personal trainer for fitness and nutrition over the last five years. The main reason for my con- tinued work with Adam, is due to the enthusiasm he has for the helping me achieve my goals. If you are committed to achieving them, Adam will help you get there! He expects nothing less than 100% commitment from you when taking part in any of his programmes. I have found Adam's knowledge of fitness, nutrition and the human body and mind to be second to none. He will tailor individual sessions to your needs and you certainly feel like you have benefited from each session."

Ricky Raithaitha (Berkshire, UK), IT Consultant

"Adam is an exceptional heath and wellness expert. Having known Adam for a little over five months now, his expertise and his ability to challenge me by getting me to ask, "Why I am doing what I am doing", has made a huge difference to my health, wealth and happiness. A healthy body and mind has enabled me to work smarter and be more productive, plus I can now lift things again as he has sorted out my shoulder pain. He is not your average personal trainer, but someone who has a holistic understanding of fitness, health and well-being. His programmes are a 'must' if you want to get more out of your workday and your personal life. I highly recommend you take out one of Adam's programmes."

Amanda Kennedy (Surrey, UK), Entrepreneur

"Adam Strong has been my personal trainer for a couple of years. The results I have achieved to date are largely due to Adam's perfect application of a combination of various training methods, individualised exercise programmes and challenging, yet achievable, goal setting. Adam's professionalism, extensive knowledge, and enthusiastic commitment to his work and clients, creates the perfect scenario for success and sets the foundation for a new healthier lifestyle! Adam is passionate about fitness and it shows through the energy and enthusiasm that he brings to each session. His easy-going, friendly personality creates a relaxed, comfortable atmosphere. Adam makes each workout challenging and most importantly fun. He also places a high value on precision when undertaking each exercise. He encourages me to push past my perceived limits to get results. I have energy and my balance and flexibility have improved enormously. If you are serious about changing your life for the better, Adam will lead you every step of the way.

Richard Rouse (Berkshire, UK), Business Owner

Dedication

This book is dedicated to my two children,

Leo and Paige,

who I love with all my heart and cherish

every moment with.

Daddy is so proud of whom you have become today.

Acknowledgements

I would like to thank a number of people for their support in helping me become a *Key Person of Influence* in the fitness and wellbeing industry.

Firstly, I would like to thank my wonderful client and friend, David Gibbons, who has helped and supported me over the years, as well as helping me form this into a well-structured book.

Secondly, thanks to Amanda Watts, a wonderful lady who has been my rock throughout my journey. She is an expert in marketing and PR, and has provided vital help in enabling me to raise my profile in my industry.

I also want to thank another awesome client and friend, Louise Walker. I don't think she really understands how much she means to me. She has helped me in so many ways, especially in encouraging me to think about my business seriously. She also introduced me to the *Key Person of Influence* business course that I have learnt so much from.

I want to thank all the other experts, including Daniel Priestley, Andrew Priestley, Darshana Ubl, Mike Harris, Mindy Gibbons-Klein, Nic Rixon, Penny Power, Julia Langkraehr, J. T. Foxx, and Jason Gilbert, who have supported me on my journey.

A big thank you also to Chris Day from Filament Publishing for supporting and believing in me, and to my illustrator, Katherine Burgess, as well as to Ricky Raithathia, client and friend.

I would also like to thank Prakash Radhakrishnan for his excellent photography.

And, finally, a huge thank you to my clients, friends and family who have believed in me and supported me over the years.

Physical fitness is not only one of the most important keys to a healthy body, it is the basis of dynamic and creative intellectual activity.

John F. Kennedy

10 Olympic Champion Winning Techniques for Building a Gold Medal-Worthy Business

Fit Body
Fit Business

Adam Strong

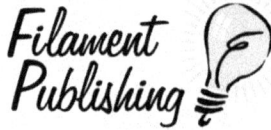

Published by
Filament Publishing Ltd
16 Croydon Road, Beddington Croydon,
Surrey, CR0 4PA, United Kingdom.
Telephone +44 (0)20 8688 2598
Fax +44 (0)20 7183 7186
info@filamentpublishing.com
www.filamentpublishing.com

© Adam Strong 2017

ISBN 978-1-911425-15-1

Printed by IngramSpark.

Contents

Foreword by Sharon Lechter

Over the past 30 years, I have had the honor and privilege of working with a wide range people to share the importance of financial literacy and entrepreneurship. I've worked with US presidents, senior business leaders, multi-millionaires, business owners both established and just beginning, and families just wanting to purchase their own home and do the best for their children.

My focus has always been on helping people achieve real and sustainable results. Along the way however, my own focus was so business centric that I sacrificed taking care of my own health. And this has led me to the recognition that underpinning all success and achievement in life is our health. Without our health we have nothing. Many people sacrifice their health to create wealth, which is clearly a broken formula. They realize at the age of 50 or 60 that all the wealth in the world cannot reverse a lifetime of unhealthy lifestyles.

I was introduced to Adam while I was speaking in the UK and learned that he had helped one of my students, Camilita Nuttall, turn her event called the 'Event of Champions' into a great success. After spending some time with him and getting to know what he stands for and what drives him forward, I discovered him as a results-orientated entrepreneur and that his experience as a former elite athlete helped him apply the same ethos to his everyday life. Adam loves to help people and combines his great understanding of people's health needs with deep business insight to offer a unique formula for success - a formula that applies whether you're starting out in your career, you're a budding entrepreneur or you're running a multi-national organization. Adam is passionate, energetic, focused and a force to be reckoned with!

I'm a great believer that, if you want success in life, a sure way to get there is by helping others achieve their goals. Adam Strong is living proof of this philosophy. He walks the talk. What he shares in his book is based on simple strategies, formulas and exercises that have worked in his life and with his clients. Adam can help address areas of your life from physical fitness and diet to mental health and emotional wellbeing. Adam will also help you articulate, plan and structure a program. If you follow the advice given, I am confident that Adam's strategies and exercises will help you achieve optimal performance.

What I really like about this book is that it offers solutions to a whole array of different issues that can afflict us in the modern world - stress and burn-out, negative thinking and low energy, living ONE BIG LIFE, lifestyle challenges such as poor diet and excessive drinking, and physical problems, such as poor posture. This book is ideal for everyone in business today, whether you're a senior executive, budding entrepreneur or starting out in your career, or a human resources director or someone running their own company.

'Fit Body Fit Business' is an operator's manual that empowers you to 'own' your health choices, wants and aspirations. As I have learned through my 4 decade career, our health is largely what we make it. It's down to the everyday decisions and choices we make. Those choices, good or bad, establish the habits that make us who we are today. From what to eat and whom we spend time with, to physical exercise and how we feed our minds, it all shapes our health and wellbeing. But the good news is that change is within you.

Reading Adam's book, has helped me focus more attention to my own health habits (or lack thereof!) and increased my awareness of how important it is to pay attention to the choices we make each and every day.

This book provides the detailed action plan that will help you create positive change in your life. Take advantage of this book, use it as a guide to create the success you want. If you do this, I know you will get the most out of your life and achieve the success that you so richly deserve.

Sharon Lechter, CPA CGMA
Entrepreneur, Author, Philanthropist and
Financial Literacy Authority

Take care of
your body.
It's the only
place you have
to live.

Jim Rohn

Introduction

You're probably thinking why a personal trainer like me is qualified to write a book on increasing productivity in your business. Well, first of all, I'm no ordinary personal trainer! I'm regarded in my industry as a problem solver, athlete, coach and entrepreneur. Apart from my qualifications and experience in the fitness industry, I'm writing this book from the perspective of both employer and employee. The biggest assets in any business are the people that make up the company, so it makes sense to know how to maximise their productivity whilst keeping them happy, healthy and engaged.

This book is designed to help you answer one main question:how can you get your employees to buy into your way of thinking? This book is an empowerment tool to give employees the answers to many of the issues that affect their personal and professional lives. In addition, it is also a tool for employers to be able to create a positive work culture. It can be used to complement an employee's benefits package, or as a wellbeing or employee engagement programme. I want to offer you the advice and support that I've been privileged to give to my personal clients over the years. This includes some great tools for change, and a proven technique to help your employees become less stressed and more productive.

My aim is simply to help your employees make a unique change in their lives, offering a practical approach to lifestyle changes, focused on real solutions to real problems. And reflecting this practical approach, there are a variety of tasks and challenges throughout the book that I encourage your employees to complete to help them get the most out of their reading.

Where I'm coming from....

I am eternally grateful for those people in my life who have helped me reach the top of my game. I'm in great shape both mentally and physically plus I have the personal freedom to choose what I do, how I do it and when I want to do it. But it certainly hasn't always been easy and I've had to overcome a number of obstacles in my life.

Growing up was tough. My parents separated shortly after I was born and we struggled financially. I developed alopecia at the age of eight and was regularly bullied at school. This had a massive impact on my self-confidence, self-esteem and relationships. Nevertheless, a bright spot was that right from my earliest years, I've always been a keen sportsman. I started long-distance running at the age of 11, progressing to become one of the youngest and most promising athletes in Surrey. At the age of 13, I decided to join my local athletics club where I trained with Mo Farah who became a good training partner. Long-distance running and athletics offered me the opportunity to escape from my family problems and allowed me to succeed at something and feel good about myself. Unfortunately, in my teens, life-issues started to interfere as I lost my focus. My mind-set changed and I no longer believed in myself. I wanted to be the best but I simply didn't have the willpower or encouragement and support from others around me to enable me to stay focused and maintain and develop my sporting potential.

I became someone who just followed the herd. I left school at 16, beginning work at McDonalds where, against the odds, I knuckled down and progressed to Assistant Manager. But, after a number of years, I felt I was becoming part of the McDonalds 'wallpaper' and might end up working there forever! I realised that my dream was not to work in fast-food for the rest of my life, but to pursue my dream career instead!

I realised that there was only person who was stopping me from doing something with my life and being a success. Me!! By sorting out what I really wanted from life, I began to turn my life around. I found my way back into cross-country running and, through a combination of self-belief and self-discipline, I got my dream job on a cruise ship - a far cry from my previous existence. Since then, I've completely transformed my life, progressing to become a recognised leader in the health and fitness industry. Now, as I continue to grow my career, it's my purpose to help inspire and empower others to succeed and achieve their dreams.

But for many people in today's pressurised, highly competitive business world, the dream that we can live our lives on our own terms is fading away. Tough economic conditions and a 24/7-business culture mean that however successful we become, we have to work harder still, putting in longer hours and taking on more responsibilities. All this comes at a cost!!

It's a fact that people living highly pressurised working lives are likely to die ten years earlier than those in less demanding roles. There is a strong correlation between lifestyle diseases and exhausted and burnt-out employees (Van Gaal L et al 2006, Cerrello and Motz 2004).

Many people simply take their health for granted and push their body to its limits. I've known individuals have heart attacks at the age of 54. Three out of four clients who come to me suffer from high blood pressure, and many are either border-line type 2 diabetic or already suffer from the condition.

To be diagnosed with a serious illness that you'll have to live with for the rest of your entire life is not just frightening and shocking - it's a game-changer. While declining health will eventually affect us all, we do have the power and the choice to make sure we stay healthy and fit for as long as possible. Now is the time to do something about it before it's too late!

You weren't born to work, you were born to live!

This book is a wake-up call. Health is your No. 1 priority - that's a fact!!

In these pages, you'll discover that there is light at the end of the tunnel and that you can achieve the 'sweet spot' in your life. I aim to give you and your team the means to re-energise your mind and body. So step-up and act before it's too late!

Be aware that this book is designed to challenge you. It sets out a number of questions you need to ask yourself and the key activities you need to follow through on. To get the maximum benefit, ideally you shouldn't move on until you've completed each question or activity in turn, but if you're unable to do this, do make sure you go back afterwards to complete each exercise. The questions and activities are designed to challenge you and get you thinking by pushing your 'hot buttons' to create the solutions for a healthy lifestyle. The book sets out a pathway for establishing a work/life balance that hopefully will meet your needs, no matter what challenges or obstacles you face. The aim is to get you living your life as you want it to be.

You might want to read it again!!

This book is not a magic pill, nor is it a quick-fix solution. It requires you to make an investment in both your own and your team's health and wellbeing. My approach is holistic, incorporating steps for creating a healthy lifestyle, dealing with excess stress and making your life that little bit easier. This book will help you and your team assess your own health and fitness needs, identifying problems and providing you with the solutions to fix them.

Your day-to-day health is very much a reflection of the way you live your life. I'll give you tips on how to get a good night's sleep, how to put stress management techniques into practice and how to deal with negative thinking. We'll also cover your ego, motivation and self-esteem. I'm going to challenge you to start your lifestyle transformation today. The book will help you formulate a plan - a workable approach that many business owners don't normally have access to.

But to get the most out of the programme, it's vital that you engage fully and act on the recommendations and tasks. Throughout the book, you'll also see that I do recognise that making such lifestyle changes isn't always easy - so I do aim to make the programme workable and build in some 'give and take' - just like being in a relationship!

Finally, you will be given the opportunity to 'step up' and make an action plan. This will include introducing high-quality nutritious foods into your diet and building a realistic exercise programme. We'll aim to change the way you think about your life, creating a more youthful, vibrant you in the process. After all, you're only as old as you think you are!

Most importantly, all readers of this book should realise that fitness and wellbeing aren't just for 'other people'. They are achievable by anyone. But you do need focus, belief and discipline.

I'm confident that reading this book will give you the opportunity and means to change your life and live the type of life you want. Not only this, I believe the changes you make will positively impact the lives of those around you.

Good luck and I hope you love reading my book!

Adam

Chapter 1: Preventing burnout

My years of experience in the fitness and wellbeing industry have shown me that clients come to me because they are ready to make a change and in a position to do so. So it's important to understand the perspective of the employee. Successful leaders accept they are not superheroes and that understanding every employee's frustrations and personal and professional challenges is difficult, especially in larger organisations.

Put yourself in the shoes of your employees. Most business people find their working life stressful at the best of times. And often as we progress in our careers, we have to cope with higher and higher stress levels day-in, day-out. Have you ever had the feeling that the pressure is too much and that something needs to give?

Stress in the workplace is commonly caused by excessive demands, impossible deadlines and long working hours (Chapman L 2012). Employees have to have the tools to deal with the high pressures of corporate life in an increasingly competitive environment. Just as important, they need to maintain their earnings potential and continue to be recognised as the best person to do the job. My question is what would happen if you felt like you couldn't meet those demands or live up to those standards, or if you felt your boss wasn't giving you the credit that you deserve? Have you run out of ideas about how they can be the best and ensure their success? Well, I hope not!

Stress is the body's method of reacting to a challenge, whether it be physical or emotional. Stress can be good if it's short-term but the problem occurs when the stress becomes too much, for a long period of time, and we're overwhelmed with the pressure, meaning your coping mechanisms won't be able to sustain an optimal level of productivity. The fact is that the most successful business leaders use lifestyle management methods to enable them to become even more productive, energetic and focused. Based on this approach, I work to help my clients explore some of the reasons why their teams think they're not as successful as they could be, how to unlock their full potential as a successful business leaders, and to identify those techniques that have or have not worked for them in the past.

Have you ever had an experience where you simply have nothing left in the gas tank? Where you were running on empty or felt you needed to recharge your batteries? Burn-out is a condition of emotional, physical and mental exhaustion, caused mainly by prolonged and relentless periods of stress. Becoming burnt out significantly reduces you capacity to function, affecting both your productivity and your ability to deal with new challenges. You may have felt useless and even resentful towards your colleagues, family and friends. But still you had to keep going, focusing on your end-of-year bonus, keeping your shareholders happy and, of course, keeping everyone in your team happy. It may be that things had reached such a level that you really didn't care about life. You may have felt isolated or simply beyond caring.

Story: A few years ago I met a young stockbroker who had been in the industry for about four years. I asked him what life was like being a stockbroker. I thought his response was going to be that he loved earning lots of cash and enjoyed his life with his expensive cars and big house, but I was quite surprised by his response. He told me that life on the trading floor was extremely stressful; he told me that he and his fellow stockbroker peers had to find ways to adapt to the daily stress of making big financial decisions that involved winning and losing huge sums of money for their clients. He felt great making money but felt terrible about losing money that wasn't his. In fact, he said that the more experienced

stockbrokers became, the less financially motivated they became towards earning lots of money. In just a short number of years, many stockbrokers experienced 'burnout' and left.

Running a business may make you feel like you're just a cog in a machine or 'going through the motions' each day.

Your routine may look like this: get up after an awful night's sleep at 5.00am, reach for multiple caffeine fixes without any breakfast, catch up with emails, grab your bag and out the door at 6.30am. Catch the overcrowded train at 7am, have a sandwich at lunchtime whilst still at the computer, finish work at 6-7pm. Then get home around 8pm, eat a large ready-meal, catch up on emails again and then get to bed by midnight. This is the reality for many business owners or decision makers; burnout is a real problem so you need to be aware of the warning signs. You may feel paranoid and withdrawn at times, which can often lead to isolation and no sense of control. You may feel overworked and undervalued in your organisation. From my personal experience, it can often feel very lonely at time.

It's not uncommon for people, such as business owners, senior and middle managers and executives to work 60, 70 or 80 hours a week. This is understandable as your commitment and sense of responsibility can make it difficult to say 'no'. Your lifestyle can seriously be affected and there can be a significant impact on your sleep patterns resulting in lack of energy and focus. We will be looking at this further in the book. You may also feel a lack of close and supportive relationships. Self-doubt may start to creep in leading to a lack of motivation. Do you suffer from regular headaches, joint-pain or colds and flu? This could be because stress is affecting and suppressing your immune system.

Activity: How do you view your life and in what direction is it heading right now? Write down your thoughts.

Re-igniting the fire!!

There are a number of strategies that may help in a burn-out situation but they're not going to be suited to everyone's needs. Firstly, let's look at the mind and your cognitive thought-process. Most people will use the left side of their brain (the logical side), which can tend to get overworked. However, it is the right side of the brain (the creative side) that we must learn to nourish and build our success on. You should take a break from technology. This includes your laptop, tablet, smartphone, emails, business reports, etc. Anything that is related to work should stay at work!

One of my best clients creates home-made greetings cards as a therapeutic way to stimulate right-brain thinking and manage stress levels.

Teams need to be adaptable, which means getting access to and using all the resources available to them. Personal or virtual assistants can help organise meetings with clients or delegate tasks, so they can free up time in order for you to be able to concentrate on what's really important. Employees should ask for clarification of their job description as they can end up taking on too many additional responsibilities. Consider setting them new tasks and challenges that could revitalise their working careers. If you see them as an asset, provide opportunities for them to recharge their batteries or even, if it will be beneficial, taking on a new position.

We don't live in a perfect world with perfect people around us. If we did, it simply would be a very un-stimulating world! Stress can be good for short periods of time. All workers get stressed - that's life - but all of us react in different ways so it's important to realise that one single approach is not going to suit everyone. We are all subjected to stress in one way, shape or form. For example, there is never enough time in the day with competing work commitments and family responsibilities. In reality, all these stresses in our life can be controlled. Stress should be manageable, allowing you to be in control of your thoughts and emotions.

Would you like to know how to help your employees cope with stress more effectively?

To manage stress effectively, we must first identify the source!! Sometimes this isn't as obvious as you may think but commonly it could be work deadlines or work demands or sometimes we just become stuck and unable to figure out what the cause is. The key is knowing how to overcome those hurdles.

The source of stress is heavily linked to your habits, attitudes and excuses. What are you or any of your team members stressed about right now? And do you have control over the cause?

You may find that being in a high-pressured environment, it is tempting to opt for easy – and unhealthy - ways to cope. These may include smoking, drinking too much alcohol, over-eating or in some cases under-eating, using medication such as anti-depressants or muscle relaxants, drugs, sleeping too much, withdrawing from friends, family and hobbies or taking out your anxiety on other people, e.g. through angry outbursts or even physical violence.

Stress can have both physiological and psychological side-effects that can lead to digestive issues, such as irritable bowel syndrome (IBS) and constipation and anxiety. Our body reacts to stress in different ways that vary from person to person.

Is this the way you deal with stress? There are much healthier ways to cope but in order to deal with stress more effectively you must either change your situation or change the way you react.

My first strategy for you is to avoid the unnecessary and teach your team how to say 'no'! That means not taking too much on so that they can't handle it. Get them to feel as if they don't need to say 'yes' to work all the time. They may feel they still need to make that all-important impression but your organisation will still survive and this could be a good opportunity to delegate some tasks to other team members.

Secondly, if you have to work with negative people then help them to become more positive. Use some of your skills and experience to help overcome their negativity. I'm a firm believer that it just takes one bad apple to spoil the other good apples. You will be amazed how negative people can drain you and your team both physically, mentally and emotionally. Remember also that your other colleagues can equally be affected and sucked into the reach of the negative-thinkers.

Team task: Write down what stresses you out and prioritise the 'musts' (those things that need to be dealt with ASAP) at the top and the 'shoulds' (the less important things) towards the bottom...

For example, commuting is often a major 'stresser' for people so the solution could be to change your routes if possible, or leave earlier or later.

	Stressor	What I need to do to change the situation?
1.		
2.		
3.		
4.		
5.		
6.		
7.		
8.		
9.		
10.		

From time to time, stress is unavoidable. However, it can be managed by altering the situation. You can change things so the problem doesn't keep re-appearing. I always find that the best way to deal with the situation is to get things off my chest rather than bottling everything up. Employees need to have a human connection, someone they can speak to and trust. By bottling things up, their tension and anxiety will continue to build, but by talking about what's stressing them, you'll start to help them address their issues.

Stress can be managed, but first you must get your employees to take control and look at particular situations from a more positive perspective by learning to adapt. If you're travelling on a train to your next meeting and it's running late, use Skype or Facetime or arrange your meeting via conference calling. Instead try taking the approach of turning the situation into an opportunity by pausing and reflecting on your own personal life. I always use self-evaluation to help make improvements in my life.

Get your team to make a list of all their achievements and accomplishments, however big or small, and on both a personal and business level, then ask them to write down how they felt at the time. It could be something that is deep in their memory banks that has made a big difference to the person they are today. By doing this, they will begin to regain their sense of purpose. For example, I still remember taking up athletics for the first time, as I trained harder and harder I became better and better, which gave me the platform to be able to achieve more by building my confidence and overcoming my self-limiting beliefs.

1.

2.

3.

4.

5.

6.

7.

8.

9.

10.

Story: I have a very good friend of mine who also works in the fitness industry. I love talking about him and his life. He lives his life in the fast lane and recently he took on a new senior job position. He also started in a new personal relationship and began a high-intensity entrepreneur business course. He also had his current client base to service as well. However, in a short space of time, the realisation kicked in that these new things he was taking on were more challenging then he thought. His work was affected; his relationship with his new girlfriend was already on the rocks and he found he could not deliver the kind of service that his clients expected of him. He had taken on too much. He never stopped and he simply could not switch off. In that short space of time, his stress and anxiety levels hit new highs. He was virtually burnt out! I advised him he needed some time away so that he could gather his thoughts and prioritise his life. So he booked a last-minute holiday to get himself together. He told me that the time away gave him time to reflect and assess what was important in his life. It gave him the time to switch off and find the answers to overcoming his challenges. It also gave him time for relaxation and for his body and mind to recuperate.

"Challenges are what make life interesting and overcoming them makes life meaningful."

Joshua J. Marine

Another view that I have about stress is that it never rains but it pours! Do you ever get that feeling? Everything happens at the same time. And it's normally the type of stressful situation that is completely out of your hands. So don't try to control the uncontrollable. Just get your team to focus on the things that they can control. If they face a particular major challenge then look on it as an opportunity to grow and become stronger. If they've made a poor decision that has contributed to your stressful situation then ask them to reflect and think how they can learn from this and what they can do to change it for the better next time.

I'm sure in your business role you sometimes feel rather isolated. If so, call up a colleague or a trusted friend and express your feelings. Somebody else's input may help you resolve the situation or at least share the problem.

In the business world where tensions are high and competition is fierce, I have known employees come under so much stress that their body switches to the flight/ fight response. This is a short-term response where the body simply cannot sustain the long periods of high-energy demands that are being placed on it. In this situation, people just literally live off adrenalin to try and keep going. This adrenalin will literally help them work harder, compete more fiercely and push anyone aside that gets in their path.

These types of employees are out to survive and see everyone around them as a threat to their achievements, job, position in the company and bonuses. Any of your team can experience this response if they get frustrated and challenged in certain situations. If you have ever experienced the fight/flight response it will always result in negative consequences. You will feel like you have the power but no sense of control. You become excitable, anxious, jumpy and irritable. This reduces your ability to work effectively with those around you. Your heart rate increases and beats like a drum. You sweat profusely and it is often difficult to stay focused and in control. The intense need to survive interferes with your ability to make good decisions so you tend to make more mistakes, and accidents are more common.

Hiding under a rock is not going to do you any good from my past experience. I used to find it hard to simply switch off; my subconscious would just keep firing off like a firework display, one business idea after the other!

Managing stress can often feel unmanageable but here are some great healthy ways to help your team make life more manageable. One of the key things I do is to set aside some relaxation time. This means making uninterrupted time for myself away from the hustle and bustle without having to think about my responsibilities. Also a great way to relax and de-stress is to find some time for laughter, e.g. organise a staff night out at a local comedy store. Laughter always provides the opportunity to put a smile on everyone's face. Another way to manage stress could be on a more spiritual level. This might include lunchtime mindfulness or meditation sessions. Yoga and Pilates are also great ways to manage stress. Another method that really helped me personally is developing a routine of walking along the River Thames or in a local park. I often just sit on the boat jetty in the evening - absolute peace and tranquillity! I find this is a great way to help me relax, as I love being near water. Following your different hobbies is also a great way of relaxing. Everyone is different and all of us can find various ways of successfully relaxing.

Team task: Make a list of things that relax you and put them into your schedule..........

Things that relax me.....

When the negative
thoughts come -
and they will;
they come to all of us -
it's not enough to just
not dwell on it...
You've got to replace
it with a positive
thought.

Joel Osteen

Chapter 2: Eliminate negative thinking

What's everyone talking about days? Well, it must be the economy!! The war in Syria, Brexit, businesses going bust, the pound against the dollar.... the list is endless! With such media focus, no wonder people are ever more concerned about job security these days. Too much media exposure is one of the biggest sources of encouraging negative thinking and it also forms a distraction. It drives me bonkers! Negative thinking is similar to uncontrollable stress in the impact it can have on our lives. I find the best way that you and your team can stay focused and succeed is to limit your exposure to the media; I do this by subscribing to Business Insider which gives you short snippets of what's going on in the big wide world. As a CEO or executive you will probably find that some of your work peers can also be negative which can impact on those around them, turning the workplace into a toxic environment. I call these negative people 'Mood Hoovers'. These types of people literally 'suck up' the positive thoughts and aspirations of others – just like a vacuum cleaner! If you've ever heard of the saying 'who got out the wrong side of the bed?' well, that's a mood hover!

A few other individuals you might want to stay away from include 'Energy Vampires'. With these people, no matter how hard you try to encourage them, show your enthusiasm, or try to give them praise, you will fall flat on your face. No matter how much energy or attention you give them, they will suck all of your energy from you like a vampire. I'm a big believer if you hang with negative people, you will start to become like them. Negative people in your team will not only reduce the performance and productivity of the other people but they will also create conflict in your team, too.

Negative thought processes can exacerbate anxiety. So if your team worries about what might happen if they lose their jobs or if they get made redundant or other such bad outcomes, it will lead to a downward spiral of negative thinking. They end up worrying about things that may never happen! Unwarranted fears and doubts can zap all their emotional energy, paralysing the team and interfering with the work routine. Constant worrying is a heavy burden that will keep your employees up all night and turn them into nervous wrecks. For chronic worriers, anxiety can be simply fuelled by their own beliefs. If they want to stop worrying and being anxious, then it's important to realise that worrying is the problem itself. The problem with anxiety is that you can't just switch it off like a tap. You might try distractions, but the anxiety will always return.

Get your team get to write down any situations where they regularly feel anxiety and place them into solvable or unsolvable columns. Solvable thoughts are normally things that they can do something about in the present, compared to unsolvable problems that are likely to be things that have not actually happened, e.g. a worry that has developed because of a past experience. On a daily basis have an allocated time slot to give them the time to reflect and write out what options they have so they are able to have more control over the situation.

Anxious thoughts	Solvable (S) or unsolvable (US)

From the list of solvable anxious thoughts, I need your team to brainstorm their ideas to explore possible solutions, evaluate them by weighing up the 'pros' and 'cons' and then create an action plan.

With unsolvable worries, get them to think about their emotions towards the situation and accept that these feelings as part of being human. They simply have to accept the uncertainties of life. They cannot be absolutely certain about everything in life unless they're psychic! However, is it still reasonable to predict likely outcomes and whether they will be positive, negative or just neutral.

How to sleep better

Sleep is essential. It is something your body needs in order to function. Research proves that if you suffer from poor sleep patterns you can develop irrational behaviour, leading to poor judgment and decisions.

Sleep has a major impact on cognitive function and physical and emotional health. The average person needs around eight hours sleep each night. How much sleep do you or your peers get on average? One of the consequences of not sleeping regularly is the inability to focus and concentrate for long periods of time. You feel tired and exhausted with reduced spatial awareness, making you less alert. Lack of sleep has also been linked to obesity as chemicals and hormones that play a key role in controlling appetite and weight gain are released when you sleep.

One of the commonest causes of insomnia is stress and negativity. Unavoidable stress, such as a loved one in hospital or an examination, may upset your normal sleep cycle. However, once these challenges are resolved, your sleep patterns are likely to return to normal. If you travel abroad regularly for work, then jet lag can also seriously disturb your sleep patterns.

I want you to recommend these possible solutions as an alternative to medication if you or your team members suffer from insomnia or poor sleep patterns.

1. Control the number of caffeinated and sugary drinks that you have throughout the day. Caffeine and sugar stimulate you for short periods of time. You will tend to rollercoaster through the day as you experience the various caffeine and sugar surges. I've seen people live off 'energy' drinks just to keep themselves awake but they are doing more damage to their health - both physically and mentally - than they realise.

2. Keep your bedroom environment dark. When it's time to sleep, this will help the release of melatonin, a hormone that is released by the hypothalamus once it's dark. I find the best way to treat a poor sleep cycle is to find out the cause. Once identified, an action plan can be put in place. In addition, you should ensure some relaxation time for at least an hour before you go to bed.

3. Deep breathing - try this simple exercise for 5-10 minutes. Use your abdomen rather than your chest by inhaling through your nose, pausing for 3-5 seconds then exhaling.

4. One of the things that have really helped me is using lavender oil on my pillow before I sleep. This can help you calm yourself and collect your thoughts before you sleep.

5. To help your team relax and deal with stress, arrange for a massage therapist to visit your organization. This is a useful way to iron out tension and 'knots' in the body.

6. Regular exercise can also improve your sleep pattern, although preferably this should not be undertaken too close to bedtime. Try to go for a jog or a cycle-ride before you go to work this will boost your metabolism and stimulate the body.

7. A bedroom is a place to sleep so turning it into your second office or a games room is never a good idea. Move out any laptops, TVs or games machines.

8. Avoid alcohol. One drink may be fine but alcohol is a diuretic which means you will want to urinate during the night.

9. Avoid caffeine. Consuming stimulants before bedtime can keep you awake for hours so avoid things such as tea, coffee, carbonated drinks and chocolate.

10. Don't eat after 9pm. If hunger does get the better of you, try to stick to something very light, such as a piece of toast. This type of food will release a hormone called serotonin that will help you become sleepy.

11. Avoid fatty or spicy foods as they could cause heartburn, causing discomfort throughout the night.

12. Create a habit of going to bed and getting up at set times even at weekends. This will help ensure your body keeps to a regular sleep pattern.

13. In general, most people tend to have a dip in alertness and energy levels between 2-4pm. If this applies to your team, then give them the option of taking a 10- to 15-minute power nap!

Chapter 3: Supercharging team motivation

> *"The thing that motivates me*
> *is a very common form of motivation.*
> *And that is, with other folks counting on me,*
> *it's so easy to be motivated."*
>
> *Jeff Bezos*

S ome people wake up each day in the hope that today is going to have a different outcome or that their life will somehow miraculously transform itself. Unfortunately, this is unlikely to be the case. Your life is in your own hands and you control your own destiny.

Self-esteem or self-worth is simply how you feel about yourself and judge how you are doing in the areas of your life that are important to you. When we have no self-esteem, we tend to generalise, jump to conclusions and find that our lives are full of distortions.

Have you ever been in a situation where you thought your shareholders were unhappy with your performance or you were going to lose a client? These are classic examples of distorted thinking. You need to challenge such generalisations. Ask yourself, why would they be unhappy with your performance? Have you asked if they are happy with how you're running the business, or why do you think you will lose that particular client? Have you not delivered value? Have you not delivered a 'WOW' experience? If the answer is yes, then why would they leave?

Activity: I want you to write down a situation where your clients, customers or team thought you did something really well. It could have been

My page of Big Wins!

smashing the monthly sales target, landing a big contract with a client or exceeding your client's expectations. How did it make you feel at that moment?

I have a great story to tell about one of my clients, Richard, who started a new role in a new company. From years of training and coaching him, I started to notice a change in his body language, attitude and negative perceptions of life. He was reluctant to discuss his poor mood, but I finally got it out him. He felt that his work was constantly being scrutinised by his new boss. He felt he was being undermined as a professional, resulting in his low self-esteem. His low self-esteem led to a change in behaviour and he started viewing life more negatively, thinking he was useless at everything and any positive successes were just down to pure luck. As his depressed mood continued to deteriorate, his anxiety levels increased to the point where he hated going to work and he became depressed. His partner and I came up with a strategy to help him snap out of his depressed state. We used counselling and neuro-linguistic programming techniques. He realised that it was no fault of his own that had led him to feel so negatively about his job performance. Instead it was other people who had influenced his self-esteem.

Team members suffering poor self-esteem will tend to find that they don't feel particularly important and that their views and opinions are not regarded as relevant. If this is the case, think of the impact their low self-esteem has not only on their own mindset, but also on the other team-players, too. We all have days when we wish we could be somewhere else and when we wish we felt more inspired and accomplished. On those particular days, doany of your team feel that everyone around them is much cleverer, more attractive and funnier, and that they are just a little fish in a big pond? How we see ourselves can often be very different to how others around us perceive us. Your perceptions may be very different because they are based on what you are experiencing or have experienced. This is because you are emotionally attached to those experiences. By comparing ourselves with other people and believing what others say about us or imagining what they might say, e.g., "They think I'm useless...", or "I'm never going to get that promotion", you are allowing other people - friends, family, work colleagues, etc. - to decide your level of self-esteem. Your view of yourself is completely subjective. It's not based on true facts. Your business needs to have a set of values that reflect you as a leader.

Here I contrast a typical company's values to those of my own consultancy firm.

Typical company's values

1. Be professional

2. Respect others as you would yourself

3. Be punctual

4. Show integrity

5. Be Efficient

6. Strive for excellence

7. Be flexible

8. Be innovative

The values of my consultancy firm

1. Be passionate and results orientated

2. Build open and honest relationships

3. Deliver a 'WOW' experience for clients

4. Pursue growth and learning

5. Create fun and a little weirdness!

6. Build a positive team and family spirit

7. Create empowerment and human connection

8. Build loyalty with both employees and clients

Team activity: We all start to form our own personal values and beliefs from a very young age. For example, my values and beliefs include "help others first and rewards will come later", "always show gratitude", and "never allow someone to dictate to you by saying you can't do something or you're not capable of doing something".

Activity: What are your values and do your business values reflect who you are as person and are you congruent with those values? Do your company values match your employees' values?

As a business owner, I'm always seeking to improve on my own self-esteem by writing down my strengths and attributes including things such as achievements, skills, accomplishments and things I am good at. Get your team to do the same. This will radically transform your team's mindset into a more positive one. You should also get your team to write down their weaknesses or those aspects of their lives that they would like to improve, e.g., "I wish I could be more creative" or "I wish I could manage my time more effectively". You should then formulate a way to prioritise each particular area, using a scale of 1-5. (1 = where you feel something is least important in your life and 5 = the most important thing.). You can then formulate an action plan together.

We can do this by asking ourselves some simple questions such as, "I wish to be more creative to do what?", "What is it about creativity that inspires me?" or "What scenarios or problem-solving methods have I used where creativity was used?". It could be "How are we going to WOW our clients this month" or "What new services can we create to fix our clients problems?".

If you're concerned about time-management, then ask yourself: "If I had more time what would I do with that extra time", "If I could manage time more effectively, what impact would it have on my life", "What strategies have I tried to make my time-management more effective?" and 'If I had more time how would it change my life?'.

Once you put a plan into action, you can then start to develop those weaknesses into strengths. By using this process, you will find that your self-confidence will start to grow and you will start to think in a more imaginative style that will help you really begin to find out where your true strengths lie.

> *"Self confidence is the most attractive quality a person can have. How can anyone see how awesome you are if you can't see it yourself?"*
>
> *Unknown*

Most of the decision-makers that I know have high levels of self-esteem and massive egos. High self-esteem is generally associated with people who demonstrate independence and act very much as 'themselves'. As a business leader, you feel like you have great leadership skills and that you're able to give those around you focus and direction, and drive the business forward to the best of your abilities. Another great trait is developing your team and teaching them how to become more adaptable to meet the needs of the business and clients. Their ability to deal with stresses such as having no time and being under pressure to hit the next sales target are all too familiar. By dealing with these issues, you will enhance your team's mood and help support healthy behaviour and lifestyles. When positive things start to happen, such as improvements to their self-confidence, this will re-align them to striving towards what their 'real' self is and what their 'ideal' self is. Business owners and decision-makers who build high levels of self-esteem tend to have a positive effect on others. They feel less anxious about life and, in turn, are more open to change.

Projecting and ensuring a successful self-image within your organisation is vitally important. Your ego represents an internal thought pattern, which is determined by what your team thinks of you and how you act. You can develop and use ego in two ways positively or negatively. Positive ego can give you lots of benefits and help you sharpen your skills and knowledge to positively impact others and encourage them to aspire to follow you as a good role model. Business professionals who exhibit positive ego have high self-esteem and self-confidence. The negative ego means it's about you and not your team. You will do anything in your power to challenge those that get in your way if you feel your ego is threatened. You don't like to listen and most of all you hate constructive criticism which could cost you time and money. An example of using negative ego is an employee that sucks up to their boss and takes all the credit, or a leader who doesn't give praise and show appreciation to their team. Using ego in a negative way will lead you to become an insecure, selfish and arrogant person. As a consequence, you and the business will suffer, staff retention becomes a problem, people become unhappy, and your poor leadership skills will lead to disrespect and conflict.

Having high self-esteem and developing a positive ego are generally good responses to a variety of issues, such as stress, organisational change, and changes in your responsibilities or hierarchy. You can help overcome such challenges. This could include improvements to your lifestyle such as weight loss or working towards completing a physical challenge. If you're thinking of embarking on an exercise programme, the questions you need to ask yourself are where you are right now and what it is you want to achieve by starting an exercise programme.

Now there must be times where you have gazed out of the window whilst sitting on the train as the scenery rushes pass you and you begin to daydream. You're a million miles away! It's great! I recommend that you daydream for at least ten minutes a day. All you need is some clarity to focus on. That image is a little hazy and confusing at the moment but practise daydreaming more and what you want will become crystal clear. One of the ways to do this is to surround yourself with positive images and even create a vision board in the office. I asked one of my youngest clients who is a regular footballer to draw what his dream is and why it is important. He drew a Chelsea football shirt with his favourite number and surname on the back of the shirt. This is what pushes his 'hot button' and gives him the opportunity to focus on something real and tangible. He now believes that he is not just average but better than any other player on the pitch! What do you and your team members aspire to?

Team task: Get your team to create a collage of photos or draw an illustration of what your team wishes to achieve. It could be a collection of images of their family; it could be that next promotion or just an image that has a positive effect on their life.

Motivation is a desire to do something in a particular way. It's an internal force that drives people to do particular things. So what motivates you to get up and go to work? What motivates you to do give the best presentation to the board of directors on your new business idea? What motivates you to hit your bonus targets for this year? What motivates you to hit this month's sales target? The key question is, "What motivates your team and why?". Get them to use a scale of 1-10 where (1 = 'I don't feel motivated or have any sense of urgency or meaning in my life' and 10 = 'This has positive meaning for my life and is the most important thing to me right now').

1.   How motivated are you right now to find a good work/life balance?

2.   How motivated are you right now to improve your health?

3.   How motivated are you to attend your children's sports day (if you have any)?

4.   How motivated are you to gain promotion at work?

Whatever number they choose to rate their level of motivation, ensure you get their reasons as to why they picked that particular number.

Knowing how to develop good team motivational behaviours in the workplace is essential if you want to be successful. By understanding Hertzberg's motivational theory and applying it to your workplace, it will help you understand your and your team's motivation and appreciate why job satisfaction is not as important as achievement. How this works is that Hertzberg developed the theory that there were two types of factor affecting our behaviour, hygiene factors and motivating factors. He theorised that hygiene factors don't actually motivate you at all. Hygiene factors can be classified as things, such as job security, salary, work conditions, policies and procedures, and relationship with subordinates. However, without these things or if they are damaged or undermined, we simply don't have a platform on which to start building our motivating factors. Without our basic hygiene needs being met, we become dissatisfied and unhappy. An example of this could be, if the company you work for announces a takeover, the first thing people worry about is job losses. You don't get motivated if your job is under threat but you may work harder.

Motivating factors are related to more job satisfaction, positive drive, opportunities for personal growth, recognition in the workplace, your team's achievements in hitting sales targets and exceeding deadlines. Understanding these factors can lead to high motivation, high satisfaction and strong commitment. By understanding their motivating factors, you can then build your own ideas or action plan around what they desire and want to achieve.

Story: Sir Ranulph Fiennes is described by the Guinness World of Records as 'one of the greatest explorers of his time'. At the age of 65, he set out to climb Mount Everest, with his years of training, support and sheer perseverance helping him succeed where others have failed. He had devoted over six years of his life to mountain climbing to overcome his fear of vertigo, which sounds crazy for someone who is a mountain climber. But he used his time to overcome his phobia, gain a world record and raise millions for charity. His motivation was his determination to reach his fundraising targets and desire to overcome his challenges, having previously had double-bypass heart surgery.

Another great motivation theory, developed by Abraham Maslow, is the understanding of basic human needs, or as I like to call them 'qualities'. I have developed a different analogy called Adam's hierarchy of human qualities. This is similar to Maslow's theory, but I have adapted it to suit the needs of the business world. There are three main parts to human needs: basic needs, social needs and what I call growth needs.

Basic human needs cover our physiological needs, such as food, water, shelter, warmth, and sex. They include things like job security, the feeling of being safe and secure in your environment, freedom from psychological and physical threats, for example, 'the fear of the unknown', protection from excessive criticism, and also the familiarity and stability of routine. These are very similar to the hygiene needs put forward by Hertzberg.

The first part of our social needs covers our esteem needs. These relate to self-worth, self-respect, the feeling of your own competence in what you do, and the respect of others. Successful people are full of self-confidence and leadership ability. Driven people like you use Ego positively. The second part of our social needs represents love and a sense of belonging. This is something I really want to elaborate on as many successful business people have no time, or choose not to have time, for these types of social need. This is about giving and receiving love, affection and trust. Love is a word that can strike fear into people's hearts, especially leaders and key figures in a business who might worry that they could be misunderstood if they express love to their people. People often associate love in the physical form, such as romance and sex. However, have you ever been in a situation when you went out of your own way to help others achieve their goals? Or when you showed care and compassion, leading you to inspire your team to achieve great results? Love is one of the best tools you can have in creating team spirit.

Many successful business people who choose only to live to work suffer as a result. Why do you think some families suffer breakdown? Because people's working lives get in the way. You may feel that, because you are working long hours, earning lots of money and bonuses, you are doing it for your family, but the reality is that you're doing it for yourself and your Ego, which is all for the wrong reasons. Let me tell you about your negative ego in more detail because, in most circumstances, you will be stuck in a cycle between your esteem needs and your love and belonging needs. Your major obstacle is your negative ego. Your Ego is defined by whom you are as a person and is defined by your toys and possessions. You think the more you have and the more you own makes you more valuable as a person. I knew a client once who lived off her Ego and lived a very stressful working life. As a consequence, she frequently went on mad shopping trips, buying shoes. The weird thing is, in most circumstances, she only wore them once and sometimes not at all. People with big egos have the need to want more and work harder to get more. They eventually see everyone around them as a threat because they feel others are trying to take everything away from them. Ego is about you and your achievements and your mind is focused on your successes. You may believe that if you don't have a big ego your reputation will be damaged. Your ego teaches you that you are always right and everyone else around you is wrong: it's your way or no way! There is no compromise with you. The reason why you may not satisfy your love and belonging needs is because you ego teaches you to be separate and detached. By working long hours you are making that choice so if you want to satisfy these needs you have to start to live your life on your terms and make choices in your life that don't have detrimental effects on you and your family. If you are a parent, it's vitally important to live up to those responsibilities. Ego is only positive if it's used in a timely manner and not used all the time. Ego can turn negative if it is used all the time.

Adam's Hierarchy of Needs

Growth needs

Transcendence

Self- actualisation

Social needs

Aesthetic

Cognitive

Love and beloningness

Esteem needs

Basic needs

Saftey needs (similar to Hygiene needs of Hertzberg)

Biological and physiological

Positive ego teaches you to respect, love and trust others, that is key to success

Negative ego holds back and teaches you to become separated and detached from others

The last part of understanding our needs consists of two parts, one of which I call growth needs. Self-actualisation is the need to live up to your true potential. Other people's views and opinions don't bother you. You are creative, accepted in society, and spontaneous. You have found your purpose. I believe in giving something back. That's why I have been known for my charity work in the past and present. This includes raising money for orphans suffering from malnutrition, and supporting football projects in the community. I would encourage your business to support charitable causes by getting your employees to work one or two days to help out in the community. The last area of need is transcendence need, which goes beyond satisfying your own needs. It's about helping others and caring about other people, helping them achieve their potential and giving them an increased sense of purpose.

So now you should have an understanding of your own and your team's motivational behaviours and needs. Now what you have to do is collectively gather your thoughts and devise an action plan or strategy about how to get you and your team motivated.

Your team action plan should consist of getting the necessary resources of time, commitment and flexibility. Get them to make a list of things that they are good at and they enjoy. I want you and your team to identify some goals. They don't necessarily need to be massive, but they should help motivate and satisfy both the team's personal and business needs. Once you have identified these goals, write down a risk and reward. A risk is something that team members may fear or may cause embarrassment, for example, putting themselves forwards to present an idea in front of all the directors. It could be something they really don't want to do. For team members, it actually turns into a motivation. A reward could be something really simple, such as rewarding team members with an evening meal out with their spouse or an all expenses paid trip away.

In order to be truly motivated, you must first start to believe in yourself and others!!

Story: One of the most powerful and moving stories that really bring tears of joy to my eyes is the story of Dick and Rick Hoyt from the United States. Rick was born with cerebral palsy. Doctors said Rick would need to be institutionalised as it would be too difficult for his parents to give him the care and attention he needed. The family wanted to take on the responsibility of giving their son a normal life. Rick Hoyt, told his father, Dick Hoyt that he wanted to participate in a 5-mile benefit race for a lacrosse player that had been paralyzed in an accident. Dick agreed and pushed his son in a wheelchair, coming in next to last place. This realization was just the beginning of what became over 1000 races completed including marathons, duathlons and triathlons (6 of them were iron-man triathlons). In the triathlon, Dick made a special seat on the front of his bike, in the swimming stage he wrapped a cord around his waist that was attached to the front of a dingy so he could pull his son and a custom made running chair for the running stage. It's one of the most moving stories I have ever heard, but the point I'm making is that Dick believed in himself and Rick believed in his father, although everyone doubted them. Dick and Rick completed a goal that was in most people's eyes impossible, and although retired from the longer distances continue to participate in smaller running events.

Trust your feelings. If it feels right, go ahead with all your heart and don't think with your head. It's all gut instinct and having faith in yourself, faith in your goals, faith in your authority and faith in your ability to change and move forward. The activities and the exercises that I give you in this book will help empower you and your team to start that journey of change. It's your destiny, so trust the journey!! Of course, life has no guarantees so don't criticise this method before you have even tried it. But if you don't try, you will never know. It will be a case of, "Well, I could've done that, but I didn't".

Get rid of the excess baggage and drop those old and draining habits. Avoid people that don't stimulate you. Change the environment both at work and at home.

Get rid of any distractions and eliminate those negative thoughts they just hold you back. It could be watching TV, hanging out with negative people, or spending too much time on Facebook. Whatever the reason, there will always be an excuse not to do it. My big distraction is my Sony PlayStation.

Team task: Get your team to write down a list of distractions and list ways to overcome those distractions so that you can become more motivated and focused on becoming successful.

For example: Reduce time watching TV to spend more time enjoying fresh air. This could help improve cognitive function and increase oxygen to your brain, thereby enabling greater success which is key for business leaders. Reduce your extra working time outside of the office in order to take time to meditate.

$\mathfrak{Self}$-$\mathfrak{Contract}$

My goal is...
....
....

To achieve my goal, I would need to change
the following...
....
....

I am willing to do the following to make this
happen...
....
....

Others will know about the change I'm making
when...
....
....

If I don't want my plan to work, this is what
I'm going to do to make it fail...........................
....
....

Therefore, my contract to myself is...............
....
....
....
....

My next tip to increase team motivation is to set individual goals or run a competition within the team. You can recruit some great followers by simply making regular blogs about your progress and asking others how they're getting on. One of the key things is to make a 'self-contract' with yourself. Remember a contract means it cannot be broken. But, yes, it can be modified if it has a benefit for you.

Find an 'accountability buddy' who has similar goals and make sure you hold each other to your individual self-contracts. This, in turn, is very motivating. It brings competition into the process – something which can be very healthy.

The Five Stages of Change

Before I empower you and show you the solutions to take control of your lifestyle, change has to start with you. Therefore, we must begin to analyse how you are going to change and only you can do this. You must ask yourself, "What mindset should I adopt?". "Am I ready to make the leap of faith?". "Am I ready in my mind to change myself and am I going to commit to it?". The stages of change model will establish if you are ready to move forward or not. If I haven't convinced you, at least think about how you can embrace change in the next month or two, then I want you to question yourself and ask, "If not now, when?". Because if nothing changes, then nothing changes.

The first stage of change is called pre-contemplation which, in a nutshell, means I'm not ready for change and I have no intention in the coming months of changing. Really? Well if you're reading this book, then you must be looking to find the solutions that will empower you to take control - so well done! The second stage is contemplation. This basically means that you are in a position where you are thinking about change. So in order to move forward, I urge you to weigh up the 'pros and cons'. For example, if I take up regular exercise then I can lower my blood pressure or, if I go to bed at a sensible time, then I will feel more energetic in the morning The 'con' could be, if I start exercise, then I might suffer from backache or muscle pain or, if I go to sleep late, then I will feel exhausted.

Make a list of things that will happen if you don't take action

The third stage is the preparation stage. In this particular stage, you are ready to change or are planning to act very soon. You may have taken steps in the past year to begin this, for example, enquiring about a gym membership. You may need a little more encouragement to make the jump so tell your circle of friends and family about the new behaviour you wish to adopt. If you feel you are at this stage, then I would say you are ready to enroll or embark on a programme such as weight loss or smoking cessation.

The fourth stage is the action stage. So you have made that change and you have carried out the steps that needed to be taken. You will understand that if you have a goal, you will know how to overcome obstacles that could prevent you from achieving your goal. You have taken steps or made changes that prevent relapse.

The fifth stage is the maintenance stage and this is about staying on track and you can do this by reinforcing the risk and reward system. Updating your goals is important as this will keep you interested and build on your self-confidence.

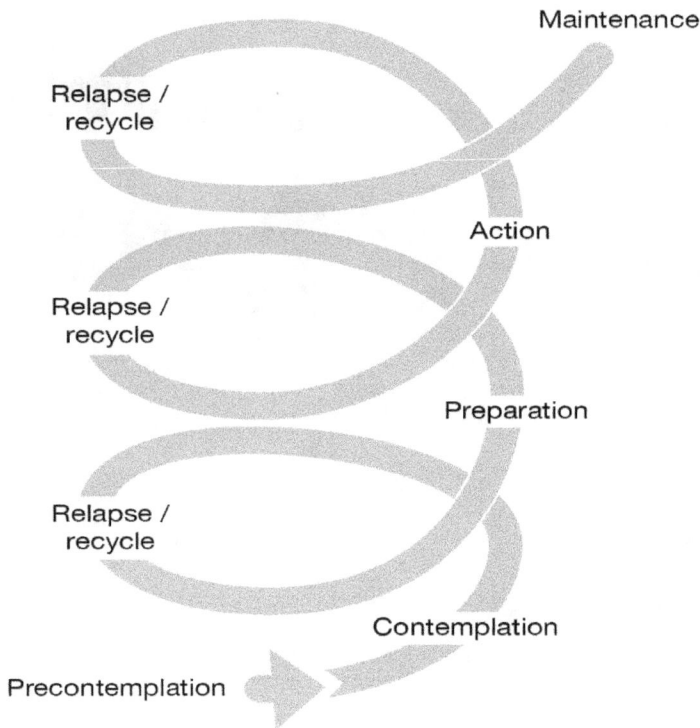

Maintenance

Relapse /
recycle

Action

Relapse /
recycle

Preparation

Relapse /
recycle

Contemplation

Precontemplation

At any point in the stage of change model, anyone can fall back and relapse at any time

So I really want to help you but you have to want to help yourself!! All of us, including you and I, have procrastinated in our lives. The problem I find with procrastination is that, because you don't have the drive, commitment or determination, you will achieve nothing. Have you ever been in a situation where you have been told in advance to get a report or a business proposal submitted and you leave it to the last minute? Holding yourself back isn't helping. In fact, it makes your life more difficult and places unnecessary stress on you.

In order to embrace change or to make that transition, you must recognise what is disappointing you about your life, and why you want to change. When I speak to clients during a motivational interview to establish their goals, I ask them, "What do you want

to achieve and why do you want to achieve it?". Most clients say things like: "I want to lose weight because I need to". After asking numerous other questions and exploring further, I establish that actually they don't want to lose weight but feel they should lose weight because someone made a passing comment. Have you ever felt like that? But actually it may turn out that a client's goals could be something as simple as they just want to have the ability to kick a football and run around with their children, but feel they are not fit enough. They are unhappy with this and don't want to cause embarrassment to themselves and their children. The point I'm making here is that in this case there is a higher motivational reason other than just weight loss. So my question to you is what is it that you really want to change in your life? What is it about your mindset, body and lifestyle that disappoints you?

Let's turn your disappointments into motivations! Make a list of your disappointments.

> *"I can accept failure, everyone fails at something.*
> *But I can't accept not trying"*
>
> *Michael Jordan*

Choose your destiny and take responsibility for changing. We all have choices in life and we all must be accountable. Forget about your old decisions. What's done is done. The choices that you make in your life right now simply do not reflect the way you are today. So make that choice.

In order to choose what life you want to live, you have to have willpower. That means you need fuel to make the engine run. You've really got to

Life has its ups and downs, very similar to a rollercoaster, but use those experiences as a learning curve even if you feel it's three steps forward and one step back.

One final tip is to learn from the mistakes you have made in the past and use them to move forwards. If something didn't work, don't necessarily disregard it yet. Think how you could modify it or improve your life or situation. Failure is not an option once you have made the profound decision to stick to that decision and not change your mind. It's up to you! The only person you're letting down is yourself, nobody else. As my mentor and motivational speaker, Les Brown, would say "There is greatness in everyone!". Now believe in yourself and make it happen!

Give a man a fish and you feed him for a day. Teach a man to fish and you feed him for a lifetime.

Chinese Proverb

Chapter 4: Secrets that your body is trying to tell you

Most busy people take their health for granted until eventually it's too late to do anything about it. In the business world, health is often 'put on the backburner' until one day you're told the bad news that could have life-changing consequences. Most of us know somebody - a friend or a family member – who have had serious health issues, such as diabetes, coronary heart disease, cancer, stroke, or arthritis, all of which are on the rise. We may be able in some instances to take preventative action through the lifestyles we adopt.

Think of the impact major health problems may have had on the lives of people you know and those around them. Do you want to suffer the same fate? Maybe you have been affected by one or more or the above health issues yourself. Good health involves not only your physical wellbeing but your mental wellbeing as well. So don't gamble with your health: prevention is better than cure. Plus good health gives you more energy, allows you to be more productive and may help you become more assertive.

In this particular chapter, I want to help you understand your body, how to assess your current health status and outline ways to improve your health. The health issues discussed in this chapter are commonly associated with people who have to work in high-pressured environments that, in turn, are exacerbated by the lifestyles they live.

Understanding your posture

I've been in the fitness industry for over ten years now and, throughout my learning, I've been hooked on helping people with their pain issues. The most common reasons why people are in pain is because of poor posture and work issues. I love helping people tackle the root causes of their pain issues, reducing the symptoms they suffer and eventually allowing them to become pain-free. Sitting up straight at one's desk not only projects a good impression, but also more importantly convinces you and others about your good health.

Did you know that at least 80% of people suffer from lower back pain? Adopting a good posture says a lot about you in terms of your body language, the way you communicate and the importance of opening and closing business deals. It's all to do with how your spine sits on your pelvis. Bad posture is due to the fact that you've sat down for prolonged periods of time, e.g., at your own desk, in meetings or in the car. Your joints begin to stiffen up, you become rigid and you start to slouch as it becomes such an effort to sit or stand up straight. Many thousands of years of ago our ancestors had to hunt for their food in order to survive. Our bodies were not designed to sit down for long periods of time. Subconsciously we know prolonged sitting is not good for us. Our muscles are insufficiently exercised and can't sustain a healthy posture.

So which posture type are you? The three most common postures I see in my clients are: sway back or lordosis; kyphosis (or as I like to call it the 'ET position'); and flat back.

Lordosis is a condition that changes the spine into an exaggerated 'S' curve. Key characteristics include:

1.   Excessive curve in the lower back

2.   The pelvis is tilted under, causing the vertebras in the lower back to move closer together

3. Carrying excess abdominal fat

4. Overworked back muscles

5. Tight hip flexor (front of the hip) muscles

6. The backs of the legs (hamstrings) are tight

7. Weak core or stomach muscles

8. Carrying a 'spare tyre' around your mid-section

9. Lower back pain or discomfort

Lordosis may also occur in pregnancy.

Kyphosis or 'E.T.' position. This condition is called the exaggerated 'C' curve. Key characteristics include:

1. Rounded and tense shoulders

2. Forward head position (your head sits in front of your shoulder line)

3. Neck pain and stiffness

4. Fatigue and low energy levels

5. Sinus issues

6. Pain in the arms

7. Slouching

8. Possibly a hump at the base of your neck. I call this the 'humpback'

Or are you a flat back with a bean pole posture? Key characteristics include:

1. Flattened lower back curve

2. Sciatica (leg pain)

3. Lower back pain, especially when sitting for long periods of time

4. Possible pain in the buttocks, groin or thighs

5. Stiff back

6. Flat bottom syndrome

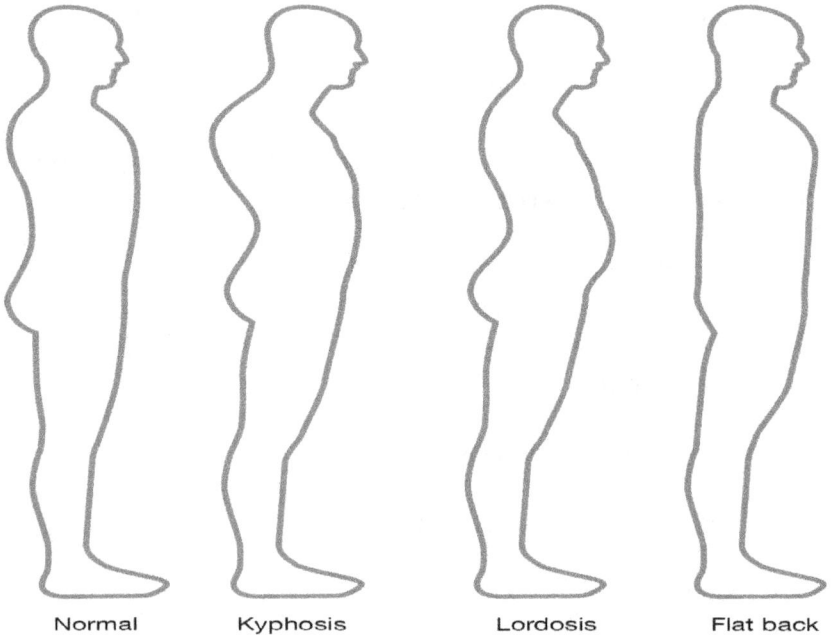

| Normal | Kyphosis | Lordosis | Flat back |

Understanding the position of your body will affect the position of your spine. Good alignment = good posture. When I observe a client for posture, I look at three viewpoints: anterior (front), side, and posterior (back). From the front, I'm looking to check that the position of the head, chin, sternum, middle of the pelvis and feet is all aligned. From the back, I'm looking at the base of the spine, shoulder level, pelvis position, back of the knees and foot structure. And finally the side view focuses on alignment of ear position, shoulder, middle of the elbow, pelvis, knees and feet.

Correcting your posture

There are two ways to correct your posture; through movement (functional exercise) or non-movement, e.g. treatment with a chiropractor.

I'm going to specifically focus on the functional aspect. I believe that poor posture is down to the lifestyle that we choose to adopt and that, in most cases, injuries occur through movement. Some people experience pain just from reaching round to grab the seatbelt or leaning over the desk. Functional movement is a great way to improve flexibility, improve joint motion, decrease or eliminate pain and improve muscular strength. I use this holistic method to get fast and effective results that last. A functional movement screen should specifically look at three main joints: the hips, the foot/ankle and the thoracic spine. I regard these joints as having the biggest influence on how we move. Throughout the assessment I look at improving basic function, i.e., walking or 'gait', and combining observation and experience to also improve posture. Choose your professional wisely. Ideally, they should have knowledge of biomechanics, i.e., how the body moves. A professional will train joints, not muscles!! I get a lot of requests about the 'E.T.' forward-head position. You're probably asking why I call it the 'E.T.' position. In the film 'E.T.', Elliott hides E.T. away from everyone. E.T. stretches his neck out to peak out of the wardrobe. That's what I relate to developing the forward-head position.

I get a lot of requests about the 'ET' forward-head position. You're probably asking why I call it the 'ET' position. In the film, 'ET', Elliott hides 'ET' away from everyone. ET stretches his neck out to peak out of the wardrobe. That's what I relate to developing the forward-head position. This tends to develop because of neck tension, weak back and poor abdominal muscles. The forward head posture then tends to create a hump at the base of the neck (cervical spine). The head is much heavier than you think; gravity pulls your head down, making the head fall forward. The head's centre of gravity shifts forwards, increasing the muscular effort that is required.

Story: Graham is 59 years old and has an important management role; he came to see me because of lower back pain and neck tension. He was also concerned about his poor posture that led to many aches and pains. His past history revealed that most of his working life involved sitting down at the computer desk. Graham had severe cervical kyphosis, limited thoracic rotation, lateral flexion and poor thoracic extension. His medical history revealed that in past years his posture affected his sinuses and his ability to breathe correctly.

Now I know that some people will think, "Well, I'll just take a pain killer or visit the GP and the pain will go away". Unfortunately, this is not the case. You have to deal with the cause not the symptoms (Cohen S 2001). Here are some great tips to help you improve your posture:

1. Adjust your driving position. It's amazing but by simply adjusting your seat position, you can have a dramatic effect on your posture, especially if you regularly drive lots of miles. Do you remember when you were learning to drive? Do you remember the driving instructor asking you never to sit too close to the wheel or too far away? If you have your face practically against the windscreen or sit leaning back, then you need to make an adjustment. The steering wheel should be at arm's length. The seatback doesn't have to be vertical, but in a position that supports your head. The top of the steering wheel needs to be at eye level.

2. Appraise your office environment. If you sit a lot at your desk, replace your desk with a standing desk as it has far more health benefits than sitting.

3. Move around. Your body was designed to move not for sitting. Go for a walk around the office briefly every 90 minutes to help mobilise your joints.

By making these simple adjustments, you will improve your posture. You'll also improve your digestive process and how the body efficiently absorbs vital nutrients giving you more energy! By making these adjustments, you put less pressure on other parts of the body and strengthen the muscles that help support the joints and aid movement. You will also find that you will be generally less fatigued and more alert. You'll feel better!

Irritable bowel syndrome

Irritable bowel syndrome (IBS) is a digestive condition. It can cause bouts of stomach cramps, bloatedness, diarrhoea and constipation. The causes of IBS are unknown, but it can be terribly uncomfortable and embarrassing when you want to go to the bathroom but can't because it causes too much pain and discomfort. If you suffer from IBS, going to the toilet can feel as if you're 'pushing a brick' or as if you need to run to the toilet every five minutes. Not only that, but with constipation you will be irregular and often have bloody stools. This may happen due to the fact your diet is generally poor and lacking in vital nutrients. In some cases, it may indicate that you have a food allergy such as gluten or wheat intolerance. If you are highly stressed, you tend to neglect your body. This can often lead to a disruption of normal function. Dehydration is very common for people who suffer from these common digestive issues. Drinking lots of tea and coffee doesn't help. Research tells us that the cause of IBS is unknown. However, studies have suggested that stress and poor digestion go hand-in-hand.

Use this checklist to help alleviate some of your symptoms

1. Eat more dark green vegetables, such as cabbage, broccoli and courgettes

2. Incorporate healthy oats, nuts and bran into your diet

3. Drink at least 1.5 to 2 litres of bottled or filtered water daily

4. Avoid fruit juices (especially the concentrated juices). The sugar content may irritate the digestive tract. Fruit juices are also calorific.

5. Incorporate probiotics into your diet. These are the healthy bacteria found in your gut that help keep your stomach health and in harmony. These can be found in products such as yogurts.

High blood pressure - 'the silent killer'

Did you know that 80% of managers and an estimated one billion people worldwide suffer from high blood pressure (hypertension)? Hypertension is responsible for an estimated 45% of deaths across the globe due to heart disease and stroke. I refer to high blood pressure as the "silent killer" as there are often no warning signs or symptoms. The causes are down to the high amounts of sodium we ingest from processed meats and foods and also to our sedentary lifestyle. Research suggests that highly pressured environments increase stress levels, which can lead to high blood pressure. Blood pressure is simply the pressure of the blood against the walls of the veins and arteries. If you suffer from high blood pressure, then you increase the chances of a heart attack or stroke or the long-term effects of coronary heart disease (CHD). If you suffer from regular headaches, migraines, dizziness, high anxiety levels and poor sleep, then these are clear signs that you may have high blood pressure. Smoking, excessive drinking, obesity, and diabetes can also cause high blood pressure.

My advice is to get yourself checked out as a precaution. If you are thinking of embarking on an exercise programme, consult with your GP first or ask a personal trainer. Alternatively, bring in a third party provider to your organisation who can offer health services such as blood pressure checks, height/weight assessments, smoking cessation programmes, etc. Most pharmacies have automatic blood pressure monitors called sphygmomanometers available for purchase. Place the blood pressure cuff around the top part of your right arm and tighten with the provided straps (but not too tight). Turn your hand so your palm is facing upwards and relax your arm, ideally resting it on a table. Press the activation button. This should inflate the cuff and, after 30 seconds or so, it should give you a reading.

The first reading is normally the high one (systolic). This is the maximum force with which the blood flows from the heart whilst beating into the arteries. It should not read higher than 130 mmhg. The second reading (diastolic) is the force as the heart relaxes, allowing blood to flow back to the heart. This should not read higher than 90 mmhg. If it does, double check and make sure you've followed the procedure correctly. Ask your GP, if you need a second opinion. The best time to measure your blood pressure is first thing in the morning, ideally before you eat anything and when you are in a relatively relaxed state. If you measure your blood pressure on a regular basis, then make sure you do it at the same time each day.

Blood pressure can be improved by integrating interval training (exercise) for a minimum of 20 to 30 minutes at least three times a week. An example of this could be 5 minutes of fast walking followed by 5 minutes of light jogging, then 5 minutes of steady running and repeating. Give yourself some variety so it keeps you interested and makes it more fun.

Metabolic syndrome/ insulin resistance

I can best describe metabolic syndrome as the precursor state prior to being diagnosed with type II diabetes. If you regularly consume sugary foods and drinks, it puts the pancreas under severe pressure as it is overworked. The pancreas releases insulin to balance blood sugar levels. This is to keep the body within normal homeostasis (normal body function). If you consume, for example, your favourite bar of chocolate or a ripe banana, your body will turn it into glucose. The higher the amount of glucose released, the higher the spike in blood sugar. If you have high blood sugar levels you may have lots of energy for a short period of time, whereas with low sugar you tend to have no energy and will want to fall asleep; you feel fatigued all the time. If you suffer from metabolic syndrome, then you may develop insulin resistance, meaning that the pancreas becomes less efficient in releasing insulin at the right time. You can minimise your risks of metabolic syndrome using a low glycaemic diet. We are going to explore this further in the book, together with other steps you can take for a healthy lifestyle. If you carry a 'spare tyre' around your mid-section, then there is a chance that you may also be exhibiting the symptoms of metabolic syndrome. Diabetes is a life-changing condition and, once you have it, there is no getting rid of it. It stays with you for the rest of your life.

Some of the classic symptoms of metabolic syndrome include:

1. Obesity and abdominal fat: more often or not your appearance gives this away. Your body shape is basically shaped like an 'apple'.

2. High blood pressure: this could include dizzy spells, regular headaches, shortness of breath and blurred vision

3. High cholesterol: this is when fat clogs up your arteries. Completing a simple blood test with your GP can test for this.

4. High blood sugar levels: by testing your blood sugar levels regularly, you can monitor the amount of sugar in the bloodstream. A simple pin-prick test to monitor this can be done through your GP, or ask your pharmacist for options. Regular exercise can help regulate sugar levels more effectively by burning up excess sugar levels and helping you burn fat.

5. Gout: if you suffer from regular gout, this is a classic sign of having raised sugar levels. Gout includes swelling, inflammation of the ankles, wrists and other joints. Gout can be very painful and uncomfortable. Tenderness, redness and pain are common.

I'm going to give you lifestyle 'first aid' and show you how to achieve the perfect body.

The point I'm making with regards to your health is that it should be a top priority. Think about it. Where would you be without your health? You can't earn as much money, you can't be as successful and you can't be as competitive. Your health affects you, not just physically, but mentally as well.

Chapter 5: Becoming extra-ordinary

In this particular chapter, we are going to explore who you are today (your current real self) and how to achieve your ideal self (the person in the future). The real self is described as who you are today in the present. It is about the way you feel about yourself when you look in the mirror. What do you see? Do you feel tired and fatigued or full of energy? How do you feel your life is going right now? Do you love your life or do you feel like you are letting others down?

Understanding your real self is about understanding the way you look. Are you happy with the way you look? If you look in the mirror, what do you see? How do you compare how you look with how other people's appearance? What is the best way that describes the way you look?

The real self also consists of describing the way you think. Do you need direction or do you like to lead? Do you need more knowledge or want to share more knowledge? Do you think by working long hours you are making your family happy?

How do you feel about the way you act? Do you feel that people see you as too serious or someone that can have a laugh with? How do you act around work colleagues and your family? Do you act differently? If so, how and why?

As you can see, there are lots of questions to ask yourself.

Write down, in as much detail as you can, how you feel, look, think and act around people. From your perspective, also describe your personality. Are you an introvert or extrovert? Are you a good listener, outgoing, competitive, and approachable? Whatever it is, write it down.

The ideal self is someone that you want to be. It is an image that you have developed over a period of time. From your life experiences, you will begin to evaluate what you have learned from life.

To help you create that image, I want you to think of someone who you admire. It could be a player from your favourite football team, it could be a politician, a celebrity, an entrepreneur, a mentor or a family member, etc., etc.

In as much detail as possible, write down what you admire about the person you've chosen. What do you see that others don't? Why do you admire them? Is it their fame and fortune or how ruthless they are in the boardroom, or how caring they are towards others?

One of the people I most admire is Sir David Attenborough. The main reason for this is I love his appreciation and understanding of nature. His knowledge has helped preserve endangered species and increased our awareness of the different threats to our planet. This gives me the drive to want to learn more about how I can help preserve our planet for our descendants - and re-align my real self to my ideal self of the future.

Now looking back at what you have written down about yourself and your personality, how does it compare to the person you most admire? How far are you from achieving that ideal self? What can you do to make improvements to get within reach of achieving your ideal self?

If you want to move towards positive growth, you must first develop a healthy mind and be very clear about what you need in order to achieve that.

Here are some fantastic strategies that can be used to improve your 'Ideal Self'

1. First make a 'commitment' to yourself and be committed to achieving your objective.

2. Establish the reasons why you feel the way you do.

3. Understand what you need to do in order to change yourself.

4. Believe in yourself.

5. Set goals.

6. Have a support group.

When we establish in our minds what our ideal self needs to look like, it must be related to our core values in life. Below is another activity to help you understand those values and beliefs and why living life by those values is important to you as a person.

1. Who is the person who you most respect in your life? What are their core values?

2. Who is your best friend and what are their key qualities and attributes?

3. If you could have one more career-orientated quality, what would it be and why?

4. What are your 'pet hates'?

5. What compliments do people most often give you?

6. What are the three most important values that you want to pass onto your children?

7. If you were given the opportunity to counsel a group of students about to graduate, what advice would you give them?

8. What are your 'Top 3' values in life?

Examples of my top values that I always speak about to my children is that family comes first, be honest and open, and try your hardest and never give up.

Chapter 6: Creating work/life balance

You will have your own perspective of what constitutes a good work/life balance. For me personally, I believe it is about balancing my working life with the things that I enjoy in life. One of the things I love to do is to spend good quality-time with my children and share their achievements and experiences. It gives me a sense of being a proud parent and reflects my core values.

Another view of work/life balance is the concept of prioritising your lifestyle (health, pleasure, leisure, family and spiritual development) together with your work life, e.g., business, career and ambition. The clients that I work with often feel that their career or business should be their number one priority, and not their family. Well, this is the wrong approach! Some people dread going home to their partners because they don't want to be nagged for working long hours. Ironically, they believe that by working these ridiculous hours they are doing it for their partner. I want to give you a reality check: you're not working these long hours for them, you are doing it for yourself!!

I'm going to show you a very effective way to evaluate your work/life balance using the 'Circle of Success'. There are no correct or incorrect answers and nobody is going to judge you. This is for your eyes only! It will help identify how balanced your life really is, and it will highlight areas where you could improve the balance. Be honest and truthful with your answers and you will get the most out of this exercise.

Circle of Success

Relationships and family	Please circle your most appropriate answer
I can easily trust those that I live and work with	1 2 3 4 5
I recognise the need for support and am continually seeking help	1 2 3 4 5
I spend at least 10 hours on focused, family time each week	1 2 3 4 5
I get together with friends at least once a week	1 2 3 4 5
I'm actively engaged in ways to support friends and family, and help encourage them to be successful	1 2 3 4 5
I take complete responsibility for relationship conflicts should they arise	1 2 3 4 5
It is easy for me to make commitments and honour them	1 2 3 4 5
I'm actively engaged in learning on how to be a better spouse, parent and/or friend	1 2 3 4 5
I'm 100% honest and open with those that live and work with me	1 2 3 4 5
I get very jealous if others achieve things before I do	1 2 3 4 5
	Total

Work and career	Please circle your most appropriate answer
My goals are written down, displayed and regularly reviewed	1 2 3 4 5
I love what I do and look forward to the next working day	1 2 3 4 5
I'm filled with a sense of accomplishment and achievement	1 2 3 4 5
I'm consistently trying to improve on my strengths and weaknesses	1 2 3 4 5
I am at home with the family on time every day	1 2 3 4 5
I plan my days at least a week in advance	1 2 3 4 5
I am good at delegating tasks and activities	1 2 3 4 5
My team look at me as a great leader and role model	1 2 3 4 5
I work in a positive environment	1 2 3 4 5
I don't feel like my work deadlines and targets are unrealistic	1 2 3 4 5
	Total

Financial	Please circle your most appropriate answer
I save at least 10% of my income every month	1 2 3 4 5
My credit cards are debt free	1 2 3 4 5
I have a set-aside fund to last me six months	1 2 3 4 5
I feel that I am paid according to my value and worth	1 2 3 4 5
I have a will and testament just in case the unexpected should happen	1 2 3 4 5
I live well within my means and never spend money irresponsibly	1 2 3 4 5
I have completed a detailed budget and stick to it	1 2 3 4 5
I have a range of investments, stocks and shares	1 2 3 4 5
I have a financial plan in place for my retirement	1 2 3 4 5
I have a range of pension plans that I can get access to on my retirement	1 2 3 4 5
	Total

Spiritual	Please circle your most appropriate answer
I would consider myself a spiritual person	1 2 3 4 5
I take at least 15 minutes each day to meditate and reflect on my life	1 2 3 4 5
Other people who come into contact with me would consider me spiritual	1 2 3 4 5
I study my spiritual beliefs on a daily basis	1 2 3 4 5
I practise my spiritual beliefs on a daily basis	1 2 3 4 5
I am dedicated to growing as a person using my spiritual beliefs	1 2 3 4 5
I use my knowledge in spirituality to resolve my problems	1 2 3 4 5
I use my spirituality to help and advise others	1 2 3 4 5
I use visualisation on daily basis to help me relax and live life	1 2 3 4 5
I have a strong belief in faith	1 2 3 4 5
	Total

Mental well-being	Please circle your most appropriate answer
I read inspirational material for at least 30 minutes each day to help my personal development	1 2 3 4 5
I listen to inspirational material for at least 30 minutes each day to help my personal development	1 2 3 4 5
I have a mentor that I trust	1 2 3 4 5
All of my friends are a positive influence in my life	1 2 3 4 5
I regularly visualise achieving my goals and objectives	1 2 3 4 5
I'm always smiling	1 2 3 4 5
I regularly reflect on what I'm grateful for in my life	1 2 3 4 5
I have purpose in my life	1 2 3 4 5
I always say no to any requests or obligations that don't fit my core values and beliefs	1 2 3 4 5
I don't feel insecure in my life	1 2 3 4 5
	Total

Lifestyle	Please circle your most appropriate answer				
I have hobbies that I enjoy and I spend time on them at least three times a week	1	2	3	4	5
I take a holiday at least once a year without any work communication	1	2	3	4	5
I spend as much time as I want with my family	1	2	3	4	5
I spend as much time as I want with friends	1	2	3	4	5
I feel there is enough time in the day to balance both work and family life	1	2	3	4	5
I live life to its fullest every day	1	2	3	4	5
I attend cultural events at least twice a month, e.g., museums, opera, cinema, concerts, etc.	1	2	3	4	5
I love adventure and I'm always looking for the next new experience	1	2	3	4	5
I have a 'bucket' list of the places I wish to explore	1	2	3	4	5
I support events that friends and family take part in	1	2	3	4	5
	Total				

Exercise and nutrition	Please circle your most appropriate answer
I do a range of cardiovascular training at least three times a week	1 2 3 4 5
I do strength training at least three times a week	1 2 3 4 5
I regularly attend Yoga and/or Pilates classes three times a week	1 2 3 4 5
On an average day, I spend no more than one hour watching TV	1 2 3 4 5
I have a filling breakfast before I leave the house (not just a hot drink)	1 2 3 4 5
I don't ever eat fast-food or take-aways	1 2 3 4 5
I spend at least 30 minutes outdoors daily	1 2 3 4 5
I don't ever eat fast-food takeaways	1 2 3 4 5
I have at least eight hours of uninterrupted sleep daily	1 2 3 4 5
I'm not a regular binger drinker	1 2 3 4 5
I drink at least the equivalent of eight glasses of water daily	1 2 3 4 5
	Total

To determine the balance of your life, take all of your scores and plot them on the clock below. You must start from the centre and use the key to mark your current status. Then connect all the dots within the clock to see how much balance you have in your life. If there are serious deviations or flat spots, then you will be able to identify the areas of your life you need to work on.

Key:

Score of 5   1 notch

Score of 6-10   2 notches

Score of 11-15   3 notches

Score of 16-20   4 notches

Score of 21-25   5 notches

Score of 26-30   6 notches

Score of 31-35   7 notches

Score of 36-40   8 notches

Score of 41-45   9 notches

Score 46-50   10 notches

Please use the same score for family and relationships.

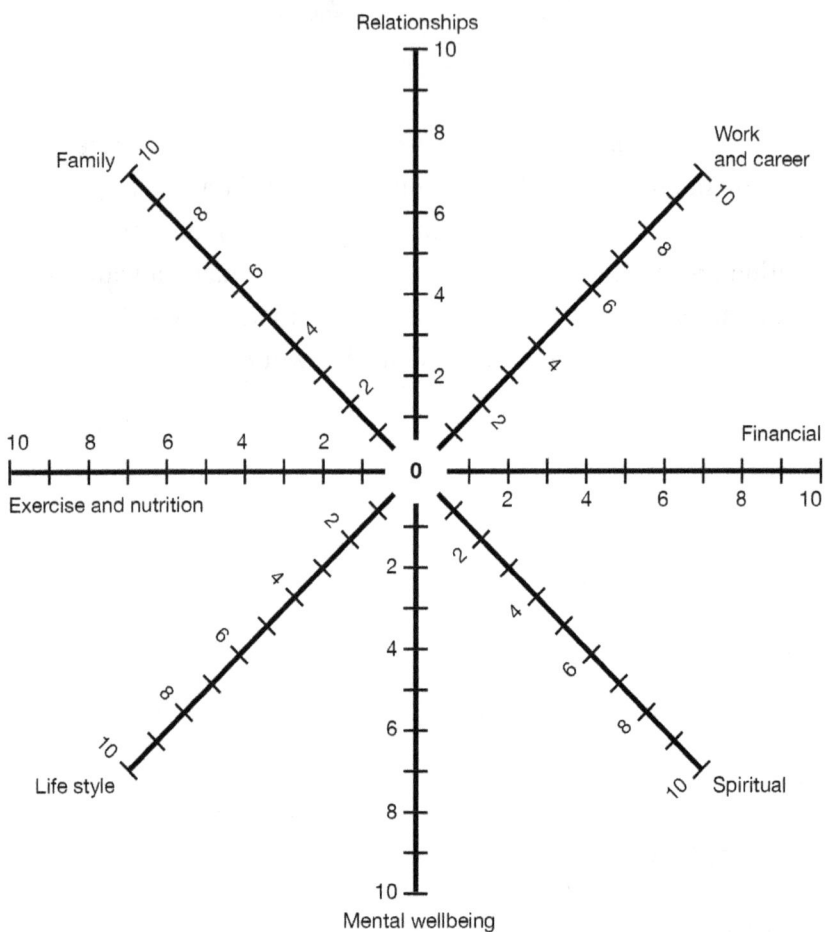

Relationships

Work
and career

Family

Financial

Exercise and nutrition

Life style

Spiritual

Mental wellbeing

I believe one of the key ways to get balance into your life is to have a good laugh. Laughter is powerful. It uses facial muscles in your face that don't get used very often. Have you ever been to a comedy club and found that when you walked out your cheekbones were aching? If you don't laugh that often, then smile. A great exercise to help you smile, especially first thing in the morning is to visualise a time in your life that made you smile or laugh. It could have been an embarrassing night out. It could have been the birth of your child. It could be that you remembered your graduation. Whatever it is, write it down.

What makes you smile? If you start your day with a smile, it will determine the type of day that you are likely to have and put you in a more positive place. This positivity will rub off on others in your team too.

So did that help you understand your life balance? Did the Circle of Success surprise you in any way? And do you think there are areas that you need to look at more closely to create a good work/life balance?

How to create successful time-management

One of the key aspects of being an effective leader is having great time-management skills. This is a science that some people find very hard. I'm sure that you have been in a conversation with a friend, family member or business acquaintance and they ask you, "How is life treating you?" or "Can you complete this report or hit this sales target by the end of the week". I know what you're thinking, "Not enough hours in the day". We've have all been there. Developing effective time-management skills takes time, experience and knowledge to achieve. I'm going to show you the tools to develop this skill.

Plan holidays in advance: living your life comes first and the best way to plan is to book your holidays in advance. The best way to do this is to purchase a big wall planner and make sure it has all the public holidays including Christmas and Easter on it. If you have children, make a list of all their school holidays. Commit to those dates and take the allocated holiday time. I always find that even a long weekend away is great way to recharge my batteries.

Effective time-management starts with your diary. Ideally have two, one on paper, the other electronic. Using a diary is a great way to plan so use it for things like attending your children's sports day, attending the gym, and business appointments. Whatever it is, stick it in. Get a virtual or personal assistant so they manage your diary and appointments. One of my preferred ways of managing my time is to use Schedule once, which is an online time management programme, so if people want to book a time to speak with me, they see when I'm available and pick a time that suits them.

I'm going to be talking about goals later but having goals is very important as they give you purpose, focus and direction. An action plan is key to strategising. It will guide you in achieving your goals and objectives, and set out when you are going to achieve them by.

Feeling overwhelmed and that you don't have enough time can be quite common. My advice is to get into the office at least 10 minutes early. By getting in early, you don't fall behind with your schedule and you can avoid unnecessary stress. So start with the small changes. They can make a big difference!

Sometimes it's hard to delegate because you feel you are the only one who can complete a particular task to the high standards you set. You believe that you are the only one who can do the task. One of the key qualities to being a successful leader is to trust in your belief in others. If you feel that someone else could do a particular task to a high standard, then delegate it to them. By putting trust in others, you empower them and build successful relationships. You should understand that everyone has the same 24 hours as everybody else, so it makes sense for you to focus on growing the business and not micro-managing the organisation.

A muscle is like a car.
If you want it
to run well
early in the
morning,
you have to
warm it up.

Florence Griffith Joyner

Chapter 7: Being fit for business

Movement is an important part of increasing energy management. Humans were engineered and designed to move. Millions of years ago our ancestors had to hunt animals, forage for roots and berries, and basically live off the land in order to survive. In the industrial age, people still had to perform labour-intensive tasks, such as mining and working in factories. Now as we move into the information age, our lifestyle and job habits have changed remarkably as manufacturing and work activities increasingly rely on technology and computers rather than the physical strength of people.

Society today is now adapted for our convenience in order to make our lives easier. You can purchase your shopping online with a click of a finger without leaving the house or pay all your bills without having to step into a bank anymore. The internet has changed the way we live our lives in many ways. We are becoming more informed, but also physically lazier. So many of us in the business world live virtually an entirely sedentary lifestyle in the workplace: long periods of time spent sitting down and staring at a screen. This lifestyle is leading to weight gain, poor posture and other health problems for more and more people. It's not just our physical health either. Our lifestyles can often lead to psychological issues, such as depression. The fewer physical demands on our bodies, the less capable our muscles and vital organs become in doing their job properly.

It is so easy to convince yourself that there is not enough time in the day to fit exercise into your life. This particular chapter will examine the best ways to introduce exercise into your busy life, explain the secrets to achieving quick results in the least time possible, and provide you with the inspiration to get your body moving. You will quickly begin to appreciate both the physical and mental benefits of exercise and realise that exercise is something you simply cannot live without. So my advice is to get up and MOVE around. The human body is a remarkable machine, so use it! Every 90 minutes or so, go for a quick stroll even if it's just around the office, or go outside and breathe in some fresh air. It's amazing how you can lift your mood and energy levels by performing these simple activities. This will help increase the mobility and flexibility of the joints, which is very important since mobility and flexibility are something we tend to lose quite rapidly as we age. Additionally, these types of activity will help reduce the risk of injuries from everyday movements that we take from granted, such as putting on your car seat belt or picking up a bag of groceries. Another big bonus is that you will lose body fat more naturally, even when you're not involved in any formal exercise programme or sports. You will also begin to fully appreciate your body from the way you look and feel. If you don't use it, you will simply lose it!

From my years of experience of working in gyms, it frustrates me to see so many people still relying on fixed-resistance machines. Just think about it: you have been sitting down most of the day, so do you really think you are going to get any results or stimulation by performing meaningless tasks by sitting at an exercise machine on your back side? I hope your answer will be the same as mine, 'No!'.

Functional training, or as I like to call it purposeful training, is a great way to get started as it often mimics natural movement patterns and functions that we take for granted. Have you ever been in a situation where you have leaned across the desk, bent down to get something or reached out in order to get to something and suddenly out of nowhere you get a sharp pain in your lower back? By engaging in a functional training programme, you will get faster results, you will burn calories more efficiently, and you're less likely to suffer from those aches and pains.

Exercise One: back squats (if you suffer from back issues, then turn your toes in slightly to activate more gluteal muscles).

Exercise Two: lunge in different directions (repeat the same lunge in each directions of the compass - North, South, East and West, followed by North East, North West and South East and South West).

Exercise Three: press-ups (try a few variations with hands positioned square, wide or narrow.

Most of my clients that I work with come from the business world and I always spend the last fifteen minutes doing what I like to call 'frustration training'. I'm talking about boxing training! Have you ever watched a boxing match? It is really hard work but it offers the potential for you to increase your fitness levels twofold. Have you ever shaken a soft drink can really hard and when you open the canit explodes? Well, when you engage in boxing training, it releases all that adrenalin and pushes your body to its limits. It will not only boost your self-confidence, but will also enable you to better address challenges and perform at a much higher standard.

Have you ever been in a situation, especially in the gym, where you have developed a routine? You begin to see results initially but then, no matter how hard you work, your body shape doesn't change. Performing slow long-duration exercises is simply counter-productive and quite pointless frankly. The cortisol levels (stress hormones) increase significantly and this often leads to frustration and poor exercise adherence. Interval training is the most efficient way to burn body fat as you can often maximise your workout by burning more calories in a shorter space of time.

Examples:

15 minutes on the rower (2 minutes warm-up followed by 1 minute medium pace, 1 minute fast pace and then 1 minute slow pace)

Running, jogging or brisk walking: 2-minute warm-up, followed by 1 minute of light jogging, 1 minute of brisk walking, followed by 1 minute of medium-pace running, followed by 3-second sprints. Repeat for 20 minutes.

I suggest using an exercise intensity scale of 1-10 (1 = very low intensity. 10 is where you are pushing yourself to your limit). This method is called Rate of Perceived Exertion (RPE). Using the RPE scale, you can simply perform and maximise your workout more effectively to the intensity suited to your needs.

Warm up: RPE of 3-5

Main session: 6-9

Cool down: 2-5

In order to stay on the path of change, you must be consistent in what you do. It's easy to become inconsistent. Have you ever set a New Year's resolution and said to yourself, "I will drop a waist-size by the end of the month" or "I will not drink any alcohol during January"? But how many days does it take before you break that promise to yourself?

How would you like to be in the privileged minority of people that do follow through and stick to their promises? Most people initially get the results they want, but often they get distracted, prioritising what they perceive as more important issues. Being consistent will increase exercise adherence and raise your belief levels. Why wait until the New Year to make the decision? Why not now?

Working out at the right time is very important. It will all depend on what time of day works better for you. Some of you will tend to work out in the morning and this often sets you up for the day by giving your metabolism the kick-start it needs. Or if you're like me, you may prefer to exercise towards the end of the day. But whatever time you choose, make sure it feels right and works for you.

One of the key components of achieving your goals is a structured training programme. Having the right structured training programme is ultimately very important and is frankly essential in ensuring you get the results you want. Really understanding what weights, duration and order of exercises, and intensity levels are required is essential. They are some of the key factors you need to take into consideration when you're planning your programme. In a short space of time, you will want to take training up a level and you will begin to question if your exercise programme is effective or not. By investing in a good quality personal trainer you can accelerate those results because they are the experts in achieving wonders. If that's not an option, ask a gym instructor or class instructor for their advice. Don't feel embarrassed or intimated. Often people don't reach their potential because they're afraid of asking. Fitness professionals can accelerate your results and help you achieve them in the shortest space of time possible.

One of the most common questions that I get asked is, "How often should I exercise?". Well, I think that entirely depends on you as a person. But if you are a relatively sedentary person, then I would start with a couple of times a week. Once you begin to adapt over a couple of weeks, you will develop a good routine leading to healthy habits. Then you will need to increase this up to three times a week as a minimum after four weeks. Too many changes, too quickly, are never a good idea. It just becomes overwhelming and you will fall at the first hurdle. If I told you to increase your exercise, change your diet, cut out smoking, and eliminate alcohol by the end of the week, what would you think? Failure is inevitable. The element of change is going to take some time to get used to. You will need time to adapt to these new changes in your life. It's very hard to change and adapt if you're not used to exercising. However, you have to develop those healthy lifestyle habits somehow. My advice is that exercising 3-5 times a week will benefit your mind, body and spirit, burn excess body fat, improve posture, and increase endorphins, leaving you feeling like a superstar!

Knowing how long to train for - and what for - is important, which is why weight training is simply a must!!

There seems to be a huge misconception that weight training is only good for 'bulking up' and increasing your size. Well, the reality is that weight training will help you achieve all body composition goals, enabling you to become more defined and improve your posture.

Lots of people - women especially, -seem to think that they will turn into Arnold Schwarzenegger if they exercise with weights. It's a complete myth!! All the clients that I have trained, especially women, are consistently using a functional weights-resistance workout. This type of work-out is used by many celebrities as is often reported in the media. I guarantee these celebrities all use weight-bearing workouts. From my years of experience of working in a gym environment, the thing that makes me mad is that personal trainers these days are still using excessive cardiovascular training to try to burn off those unwanted pounds, despite knowing that weight-training creates and stimulates muscle. Muscle is key to burning fat because it's active tissue. More muscle means an increase in metabolism resulting in an equal increase in calories burned when training or not. That combination will lead you to be lean and fit and to achieve your ideal body shape. Who doesn't want that?

Building muscle will help you burn fat more efficiently. Your 'bingo wings' will be a thing of the past, your 'man boobs' will turn into a developed chest and your butt will look like a butt!!

Yes, my clients are often pushed to breaking point but, guess what, they value their results and they keep coming back for more!! They see incredible results and from what they have learned they appreciate that results can only be achieved through commitment and effort. That's what it takes to get the strongest and leanest-looking body!

Listening to music while training can be a great help in maximising your motivation. Research suggests that people are more motivated when exercising if they listen to their favourite music. One of my favourite tunes, especially when running up a hill, is the 'Rocky' theme tune, 'Eye of the Tiger'. The fact is music makes exercise more enjoyable. You will maximise your results and it's likely you will put more effort into your workout.

Another way to maximise your workout is to make sure you stick to your 'reps' (repetitions)!! We are all inclined to be a little lazy at times and if you're not being pushed, you may just 'cop out'. Laziness, boredom and lack of focus can kick in. So stick to your agreed number of reps. You will see the results if you put the reps in!

There are a number of tools out there that can help you monitor your progress. One in particular is a fantastic app, called 'Coach Eye'. It shows you, before and after your workout, exactly which parts of your body you need to work on and how effective your routine is in delivering results.

So, it's important to find a way to be able to monitor your progress – right from the outset through to the place where you are going to finish. Coach Eye is a great motivating tool that shows you 'before and after' photos. By lifting heavy weights and keeping going for longer periods of time, you will start to raise your belief levels by seeing that the effort you are putting in is paying off. Other ways include measuring your waist-size regularly and keeping track of your results in a diary or journal.

Remember by embracing change and re-energising yourself, you can use this experience as a learning journey. Explore what works for you and embrace it. Others will follow and take on board what you have learnt, but if you want to start living life, this is where it starts.

To be a great leader, you need to be able to manage stress effectively and ensure some relaxation time. By having a regular Swedish or sports massage, you can help reduce muscle tension, improve lymphatic drainage, and help get rid of toxins in the body. Massage is a great way to relieve stress and unwanted tension. You should have a massage every fortnight or at least once a month. You really will feel the benefits, helping free tight muscles, which will improve joint mobility and posture.

One of the key problems that business owners, entrepreneurs or company directors most commonly encounter is lack of time for training. One of my favourite tools for overcoming this is a 'TRX' or 'suspension trainer'. The TRX was originally designed for the U.S. marines. However, it has proven very popular in today's fitness training environment. It can provide you with an explosive workout as it uses a range of body weight resistance, allowing pushing and pulling movement patterns that are designed to challenge different parts of the body. It's light and durable, which means it can be easily transported so it will fit in your suitcase if you're travelling a lot. It's relatively inexpensive at around £200. You can use the TRX indoors and outdoors. You can use a tree or a climbing frame to wrap it around and use as an anchor point. If indoors, you can attach it to a beam or a door.

These are my top 5 TRX exercises that will burn fat fast!

1. Burpees:

Starting position: Body is in a prone position, feet are together and placed into the ankle straps of the TRX, hands are positioned shoulder-width apart, head in alignment with the spine.

Action: Keeping the feet together, drive both knees up to the chest.

2. Squats:

Starting position: Feet hip-width apart, back straight, holding the TRX with hands and elbows extended, keep the TRX taught, eyes looking straight ahead.

Action: Bend both knees beyond 90 degrees, buttocks as low as possible, feet flat on the ground, back straight.

3. Jack-knife and press-up combinations:

Starting position: Body is in a prone position, feet are together and placed into the ankle straps of the TRX, hands are positioned shoulder-width apart, head in alignment with the spine.

Action: Keeping the feet together, drive both knees up to the chest and extend the legs, then lower the chest to the ground keeping the body aligned throughout the exercise.

Perseverance is the hard work you do after you get tired of doing the hard work you already did.

Newt Gingrich

4. Hamstring curls:

Starting position: Lying on your back, feet placed through the ankle straps of the TRX, knees soft, buttocks slightly lifted.

Action: Head and shoulders stay flat on the floor, feet together, bring feet towards your buttocks whilst keeping your hips lifted.

5. Chest flies:

Starting position: Angle the body forwards approximately 20-30 degrees, grip the TRX with your hands and with the straps taught, hands positioned at chest level, head up, elbows soft.

Action: Extend the arms open whilst keeping the elbows soft.

The TRX is a great way to improve your movement patterns on your travels around the globe!

I'm going to let you in on a secret that will keep you out the gym and it goes like this... Keep your workouts short and intense.

Just like you, I too find that time is short. Even though I'm in my thirties I feel like I'm still 21. I put being in great shape down to my short, quick and effective workouts of 30-45 minutes - absolute maximum. Get in and out as quickly as possible. How does that sound?

Seven tips to staying healthy in the office

Use these tips to help you make positive changes to your own life-style and to your team's as well. They all require minimum effort!

1. Replace all desk chairs with Swiss balls. They will improve everyone's posture, preventing slouching and placing unwanted pressure on the lower back.

2. Always have a healthy snack, e.g. a bag of nuts, in your desk draw; this will help sustain your energy levels throughout the day.

3. Keep a bottle of filtered water on your desk and drink the entire bottle (ideally the water should be from a glass bottle, not a plastic one). Water will keep you hydrated and energised throughout the day.

4. Stay away from the coffee machine! The caffeine may initially wake you up, but shortly after you will come crashing down and you will be left feeling exhausted.

5. Get outside during your lunch hour for at least 20 minutes. All that air conditioning can have an effect on your skin, eyes and energy levels, so go out and get some good old-fashioned fresh air!

6. Improve your workstation ergonomics by just taking a few moments to assess the position of your desk, chair, keyboard and computer screen. All these factors have a direct impact on your comfort and posture.

7. Take the stairs not the lift - unless it's on the 25th floor or above!

In order to increase your exercise adherence, find a sport or health routine that you love. It can also help to have an 'accountability buddy'. You can push each other to succeed and you will probably also develop an element of competitive spirit to push you even a little bit further. Tell everyone including friends, family and work peers about your goals. People love to hear how you're getting on, so keep them informed and let them participate in your journey. If you want, it might be useful to join a club or form a group with like-minded individuals. My running club, for example, helps me get focused and my coach pushes me and makes it competitive. There's also a great social dimension through building friendships and establishing rapport.

If you are going to make the commitment to change your life, then don't do it half-heartedly. It's exactly the same scenario as being at work. If you set yourself a task or know that you have to produce a flawless performance in front of the board of directors, then you are going to pull out all the stops and put in 110% effort, aren't you? I believe that by putting 110% effort into changing your lifestyle, you will feel the most fantastic sense of achievement, having accomplished what you set out to do. People around you will also begin to fully appreciate how serious you are. By committing 110%, people who come into contact with you will sense and see the change in you and the beneficial impact it is having on your life.

Your diet is
a bank account.
Good food choices
are good investments.

Bethenny Frankel

Chapter 8: Good energy management...
big competitive edge

C hanging your nutrition is going to have the one of the most profound life-long effects on your body and health. Drinking alcohol excessively and over-eating foods that contain unhealthy fats and sugars not only lead to the 'spare tyre' around your waistline, but also increase the amount of visceral fat around your organs. I cannot state how important it is to re-energise your life and change your body shape. Taking care what you eat has a huge impact.

In this chapter, in particular, I'm going to give you some key points about nutrition. Most of these points only require you to make small changes, but the aim is that they become life-long changes and you adopt permanent healthy habits. Initially, before any physical training programme takes place, I aim to kick-start clients' energy levels and metabolism using detoxification. This starts to improve health, and as a side-effect, fat loss can be achieved.

It is imperative to understand that in order to achieve good nutrition there are other things you need to do in order to maintain results. This book is designed to share the work I do with my clients. It is focused on encouraging you to make key changes to support your health and wellbeing so that you can live comfortably with your body.

Oxidative stress

have spoken very much about how stress can affect your life in many ways and the impact it can have on you and others around you. One of my biggest passions is talking about internal stress or 'oxidative' stress. Your body is made up of trillions of cells and, every second, at least a million cells go through some sort of change.

The best way to describe a cell is to understand its structure. A cell is a bit like an apple when you slice it in half. What does it start to do? That's right, it start to turn brown and begins to slowly degrade. Oxygen molecules attack the apple, hence the colour change (oxidative damage). Now, it's not just the air that we breathe that can damage our cells, but also a wide range of other things. Not enough exercise, a lack of vitamins and minerals in our diet, smoking, alcohol, the environment we live in, and over-exposure to sunlight can all have a significant effect as well. None of us can get away from all this oxidative damage. It's simply impossible, but it's not unmanageable. When oxidative damage attacks human cells, we call this free radical damage. This causes the cell to become unstable, which also causes other cells to become unstable, too. Research has suggested too much free radical damage may result in cancerous cells. Did you know that every time you take a puff of a cigarette, the smoke contains at least one billion free radicals, causing damage to cells as well as exposing them to other toxic chemical substances contained in the cigarette? Smoking not only damages cells, but also accelerates the aging process by at least 10 years.

Let me give you another example related to what you eat. How do you feel when you have a fast-food takeaway burger? You may often feel strangely unsatisfied, leading you to crave more food. In addition, you will probably begin to feel sluggish and tired within a short space of time. This is free radical damage. Our bodies can repair cells over time but they must be able to cope with the workload. So it is possible to be healthy. However, we have to take responsibility for minimising the oxidative stress on the body. One of the ways of best achieving this is to eat healthy foods that are natural antioxidants. Most people know that antioxidants are good for them but generally don't know why. Have you ever seen advertisements for food products that contain high levels of antioxidants or have you ever picked something up in the supermarket labelled 'contains added antioxidants'? The best way to describe antioxidants is to imagine the sliced apple previously referred to. How can we reduce and slow that process of oxidative damage? An excellent antioxidant is lemon juice. By squeezing the juice over the apple it forms an invisible protective barrier that slows down the degrading process. When it comes to making a change, nutrition plays a very important role but we also have to understand the importance of maintaining healthy cells. Healthy cells = healthy body.

Some other foods rich in antioxidants include most fruits and vegetable, such as strawberries, blackberries, blueberries, lemons, oranges, garlic, and tomatoes. Seafood, dark chocolate and red wine are further examples but there are a whole lot more. Adapting your diet so it contains high levels of antioxidants will help give you the ability to deal with stress on a more manageable scale.

Detoxification

The best way to describe detoxification is that it's similar to getting your car serviced. Every year or every 20,000 miles your car will require a service. Included, as part of that service, is an oil change. By having your car serviced regularly, you can expect to reduce your maintenance bills and the car will last longer. It's exactly the same with your body. If you don't get it regularly serviced and the oil changed, it will become less efficient and productive. Detoxification is great if you are feeling sluggish, have carbohydrate and sugar cravings, or have a poor metabolism, irregular bowel movements and poor energy levels. Detoxification is a great tool for correcting most digestive issues, including a leaky gut, food intolerances, irritable bowel syndrome and constipation.

It's essential to commit to your detoxification systems. Being in a job where you're sitting down most of the time and suffering lack of movement can often lead to fluid retention especially around the ankles, stomach and thighs. If you're a typical rail commuter, then you will probably have long days, getting up early without any time or desire for breakfast before you leave home. Coffee grabbed on the way to work will probably be your best friend. You may also feel short-tempered, edgy, and not in control of your emotions.

An increase in body fat especially around your stomach is also a clear indicator that you need to detox!! Otherwise the 'spare tyre' around your mid-section is only going to get bigger!

Successful detoxification can also help to reverse insulin resistance as it can help remove the body's waste products and help balance blood sugar (glucose) levels.

Story: Three weeks before I completed a dissertation, I decided to do a five-day detoxification programme. I felt it was the right time and I needed a quick solution to revitalise my energy levels. I was under a huge amount of stress. I had assignment deadlines to meet, other course work due, as well as business and family commitments. I felt quite overwhelmed! My detox included low-glycaemic nutritional smoothies and shakes, low-glycaemic nutritional snack bars, potent multivitamins and omega-3 fish oils. After a week, I felt absolutely amazing - re-energised, focused, and calm. The detox gave me the means to deal with my stress levels effectively. My friends and family made various comments, such as, "You look different, fresh and invigorated".

Your liver is the third most important organ in your body. It is where the detox process needs to take place, as the liver is responsible for metabolising the food we consume into the nutrients the body needs for energy and health. There are certain things that can interfere with liver function. These include alcohol, pesticides, oestrogen (high levels of oestrogen in men can lead to the growth of breast tissue: 'moobs' or 'man boobs'), medications, refined sugar, and trans-fatty acids.

A common question that I often get asked is how often should I detox? Well, a detox doesn't necessarily need to last for very long. It can last for just five days, although some people choose programmes that continue for months on end. I would recommend that you detox at least once every six months. This will help you develop a routine of healthy eating, balance your blood sugar levels, create healthy-eating habits and correct digestive issues. Detoxing will give you the kick-start your body so desperately needs.

Here are some very simple steps for you to take to help with this process.

Phase 1:

Increase B vitamins: these types of foods contain powerful anti-oxidants. They are also known as energy foods and include foods such as oysters, mussels, liver, caviar, mackerel, lean beef, lamb, Soft cheeses (in moderation) and ducks' eggs (chickens' eggs are OK, too, but have less vitamin B12 in them).

Phase 2:

Increase the sulphur in your diet. Supplementation is not required as many types of foods contain sulphur. These foods increase immune system function, support liver function, and have anti-cancer properties. They also contain amino acids (the building blocks to cell regeneration and recovery). Foods containing sulphur include beef, chicken, egg yolks, onions, shallots, leeks and garlic.

Use this checklist to help with your digestion

1. Eat slowly and chew your food: it enables the stomach to more readily break food down.

2. Drink water in between meals

3. Eat 'real' food, i.e., fresh food that you prepare yourself, not microwave ready-meals.

4. Include probiotics in your diet: probiotics contain friendly bacteria for your gut to maintain its health and harmony. Probiotics can be found in yogurt.

5. Be regular: a well-functioning digestion system will help you become more regular. If you don't have a regular cycle, it can lead to the body holding onto unnecessary waste products and toxins.

6. Stimulate your digestion by drinking hot water with a slice of lemon in it on a daily basis.

7. Include a variety of berries, such as blueberries, strawberries, blackcurrants, redcurrants and blackberries, in your diet.

The glycaemic index

The world of nutrition is a confusing place for many people. There are so many mixed messages about what to eat of what not to eat. It's no wonder we're left scratching our heads. I remember when I was at school; we were taught about the conventional 'food pyramid', which was originally designed to fight heart disease in the 1960s. The food pyramid helped give people nutritional advice on what foods to eat on a daily basis. This clearly isn't working for us anymore, as our lifestyles are very different from those of over 50 years ago. One of the causes of the high levels of obesity we are seeing in Western society could be down to the fact that I still hear talk of the need to eat six to eleven servings of bread, potatoes, cereal, and rice daily, together with five portions of fruits and vegetables and two to three servings of meat, poultry, nuts, milk, yogurt, cheeses, with fats and oils used sparingly. This type of thinking has clearly failed society and has now left us with a major health epidemic, especially as people undertake less physical activity in their jobs. I'm going to show you my very own food pyramid that I think everyone should use. It really does work! It's called the 40:30:30 diet. That means your diet should consist of 40% carbohydrate, 30% protein and 30% healthy fats.

I especially advocate using the glycaemic index as it really works. The glycaemic index is used to measure how quickly your blood sugar levels will rise after eating a particular food. The glycaemic index is used to estimate how much each particular carbohydrate in a food raises blood glucose levels relative to pure glucose. Foods are placed in a table called the glycaemic index (GI). The higher the place in the GI, the faster the glucose gets released into the blood stream. Glucose has a GI of 100 whereas an apple has a GI of around 24. What I really love about the glycaemic index is that it is related to how much energy you get from a particular food and over what period of time.

What is your general routine at lunch? What do you buy most often? Do you tend to buy a sandwich, panini, or sausage roll? Now how do you feel immediately after your lunch and how do you feel 45 minutes later?

Write down your thoughts

Understanding your reaction to food is very important as it generally makes you aware of how it makes you feel, whether you feel energetic or not, bloated or not, or if you feel satisfied or not. By understanding your reactions, you can then make sound decisions about which foods to consume. From my past experience when I eat pasta, for example, I generally feel sluggish and I want to fall asleep. Do you ever get a similar feeling when you eat a particular food? One of the key steps you need to take in monitoring what you eat to is to keep a food diary. I find the best way to keep a food dairy is to keep track of what I eat for two days in each working week, combined with one day from the weekend as you're eating habits are likely to be different then. Write out your food diary so that you understand it. Include a description of how you feel immediately after consuming a particular food and then 30 minutes later. The point to recording what you consume is to create awareness and to get it to act as a 'wake-up call'. You need to take accountability, so if you're going to change you need to know what to eat and how you're going to change your diet.

Many of your team will relate to the following scenario: about 2 to 3pm you experience a general dip in energy. This general feeling of 'slowing down' starts to spread amongst your colleagues throughout the office. One makes a passing comment and says, "I'm hungry!". As energy levels start to dwindle, one person goes to the vending machine to purchase a bar of chocolate and a coffee, then somebody else does, then another and another, and so forth. Everyone is suddenly buzzing around. People are lively and start 'bouncing off the walls'! Have you ever experienced something like that in your work environment? Then suddenly, 20 to 30 minutes later, the novelty has worn off, energy levels dip again and it's all gone quiet. People become less productive and start staring at the clock, counting down the minutes. This is what I called the 'glycaemic crash'.

Let me give you another example. One of the UK's favourite foods is mashed potato. Now a potato is grown in soil, which has generally been over-farmed. Then you peel the potato (the most nutritious part is the skin). Then you tend to over-boil it until it crumbles, then you mash it up. Most of the nutrients are therefore lost through the cooking process. The potato is a food with one of the highest scores on the glycaemic index – 94, compared to table sugar which has a glycaemic score of 74. An alternative to potato is sweet potato that has an average glycaemic rating of just 19. We offer our clients lunch and learn sessions which have been specifically structured to help your team maximise their energy levels through good knowledge of diet and nutrition.

When you consume something that is generally high on the glycaemic index such as a bar of chocolate, white rice or pasta, your blood sugar levels will rise. This then sends a message to the brain, and then to the pancreas to release insulin in order to return blood sugar levels to normal. However, when the pancreas releases insulin, it doesn't know how much to release, and it can often release too much insulin as a consequence. I call this 'the overspill'. As a result of the overspill, blood sugar levels drop rapidly below normal levels. This then triggers hunger and 'carb cravings' kick in.

You will most likely make a decision either to eat something else that will satisfy your hunger or alternatively be disciplined and not eat at all, forcing the body to release two hormones, adrenalin and cortisol (stress hormones) to balance your blood sugar levels. If you decide to eat something carb-based, then this creates a 'rollercoaster' effect whereby you get 'highs' and 'lows' throughout the day, leaving the pancreas overworked and exhausted. If this is you, then be aware that one day your pancreas will give up on you. That's a fact and you may become diabetic for life.

Many people working in offices may tend to be overweight and the main reason for this is insulin, which is what I call the fat hormone!! So insulin makes you fat. But one other factor is stress. Stress can keep your blood sugar level elevated, due to high levels of cortisol and adrenalin.

The key point I'm trying to make is that, if you want a more sustained source of energy, then choose low glycaemic foods and avoid high glycaemic foods. If you are conscious of your weight, don't be too concerned about your fat consumption but check your sugar consumption. The UK government's daily guideline is 100g.

When clients come to me asking for help, I always ask them if they are going to embrace the changes I suggest for them. As part of this, I always ask them to create a food diary at the beginning of my programmes. With your typically high-pressured and stressed lifestyle, it's vital that you acknowledge that your mind, body and nutrition come first!! I always ask clients to write out their food diary for two days during the normal working week and for one day during the weekend. This in most cases is a big wake-up call. I believe that 70% of the health improvements that you need to make can simply be achieved by changing your nutritional habits. With your food diary, you can see where you are going wrong and then start to make improvements.

If you're going to follow my advice about the glycaemic index and try to sustain energy levels over a long time-period, you are going to need to 're-fuel' every 2 to 3 hours. Your metabolism is key to burning fat the natural way. If you have a high metabolism, it will be easier for you to burn calories when you not exercising at all. Who doesn't want that? If you go for long periods of time without eating, the body will need to find an additional energy source to feed off, which is muscle. Muscle helps because it is active tissue. The more muscle we have, the leaner we will look. So don't let your metabolism drop: that's key or your body will start to eat itself and you will hold onto your excess fat.

There is an important window of opportunity to fire up your metabolism and this is normally first thing in the morning. After sleeping for a long period of time without food, your body will be craving its first 'fuel'. Fire up your metabolism and keep the fire alive by regularly re-fuelling throughout the day! This will turn your body from a sluggish fat-storage warehouse into a natural fat burning machine. If you want to achieve the body of your dreams, my advice is to never go hungry!

One of the other things that you need to consider very seriously is alcohol intake, even after a detoxification process. Alcohol is not only calorific but it will also prevent you from burning fat. It also interferes with the function of the liver. Throughout my initial 12-week programme I tell my clients that, although it's not forever, if they are serious about the programme and change, then no alcohol. Experience has shown me that clients' body shape and lifestyle will only improve if alcohol is removed from the equation.

As part of the detoxification process, I have a list of rules throughout the programme and one of these is cutting down on caffeine. You are probably stressed enough and by drinking caffeine you are simply making your symptoms worse.

Story: A friend of mine is really into martial arts. However, his job as a sales executive comes with huge responsibilities and stress. He lives off Red Bull. He probably drinks at least five or six cans a day. This increases that nasty hormone, cortisol, that I was talking about. He believes that drinking Red Bull keeps him alert. Well, actually, I would say he is becoming a sugar addict. The stimulants and the huge sugar content of energy drinks can get you hooked in the same way that a heroin addict needs a constant fix. Increased cortisol = increase fat levels and an overworked pancreas. Insulin makes you FAT!!

If you're a regular coffee drinker and think drinking decaffeinated coffee is a better option, then unfortunately that's not the case. Decaffeinated coffee generally contains toxic chemicals. My advice is to swap your coffee or energy drink for a green tea, or red bush or peppermint tea, or just stick to water!! In the evening, camomile tea can also be very good for de-stressing. Cutting out caffeine may seem quite hard initially, but it is well worth it and you will benefit both mentally and physically.

Eat lots and lots of dark, green leafy vegetables. Not only are they nutritious, but they're also full of antioxidants. Green leafy vegetables include spinach, asparagus, Savoy cabbage, curly kale and broccoli. The best way to eat them is raw. Nutrients can be lost through the cooking process.

One of the questions I get asked most about is supplements!! Some people and even health professionals say that you simply don't need to take supplements. You can get all your nutrients from your food. Well, that simply is not the case anymore. Times change. An orange these days contain fewer nutrients then it did thirty years ago. An increase in the use of pesticides and fertilisers, over-farming, plus reliance on greater amounts of imported fruits and vegetables, especially in the UK, means our food loses vital nutrients. We should all take supplements even if we eat a totally organic diet. Supplements are there to complement a healthy diet, not replace it!! I always carry out an initial lifestyle appraisal for my clients and, in all cases, they are lacking essential vitamins and minerals.

The first supplement that I recommend taking is Omega-3 fish oils, not cod liver oil, which some people think is the same. Additional Omega-3 in your diet will supply you with an additional energy source from the 'healthy fats' it contains. Omega-3 also aids brain function and helps reduce inflammation (especially that caused by exercise), and increases focus and concentration levels. However, the biggest benefit is that it helps fight stress. Everyone that I have trained has seen positive changes within the first two weeks of the programme. Omega-3 is contained in oily fish, such as mackerel, sardines and kippers. However, you need to consume a minimum of three servings of oily fish weekly to benefit fully.

For general health, I consider multivitamins 'a must', especially those that include a wide range of different vitamins and minerals. However, you should be very cautious about which multivitamins you purchase. There are some key questions you need to ask yourself. Are they potent? Are they third party-tested? Have they been tested for purity? Do they meet pharmaceutical standards? Read carefully what each multivitamin tablet contains and how it is manufactured, etc. Three out of four supplements are contaminated and may contain harmful and banned substances, such as lead and mercury. So do your research (Fox 2010).

Check out this website - adamstrong.usana.com - and fill in the free health assessment online. It will provide a personalised and customised assessment of your various nutritional requirements. The products I recommend are free of contaminants and also made to pharmaceutical standards.

Eat only until you feel satisfied!! That's the not the same as feeling like a stuffed pig! In certain situations, especially if you have been invited to a meal, many people feel obliged to eat everything on the plate. Don't feel like that!! Eating too much is a main reason why people are becoming fatter. In Western countries, especially in places like the United States, portion sizes are humongous. Many of us no longer know when to stop eating, with food often becoming an addiction. Your body can only absorb a certain level of nutrients from food at one time, the rest is stored as excess body fat. Typically people with busy working lives often develop the habit of consuming large amounts of food in one 'hit', normally as a large evening meal. However, your energy levels and metabolism cannot be sustained through this method.

When thinking about the food you buy, think 'organic'! Although organic foods may cost a little extra, they are still excellent value as they can contain up to five times more nutrients and antioxidants. If, like me, you have a love for 'supercars', think of the most beautiful and elegant Ferrari or Lamborghini you have seen: it's shiny and glossy and the engine roars. When you fill the tank up, you're not going to fill it up with poor quality fuel, you're going to fill it with the best! It's exactly the same with your body. The best fuel will work to keep your body operating at the optimum level. Look after your body and it will look after you!

Some organic foods can sometimes be very hard to get hold at certain times of the year. However, there are two essential organic foods - eggs (ideally omega-3) and chicken - which are normally always readily available. If, however, organic produce is unavailable, always go for the next best thing, which is free-range.

Have you ever heard the saying, 'Breakfast is the most important meal of the day'? Well, it's true. Ensure you eat breakfast and set yourself up for the day! Avoid the temptation of relying on a series of frequent caffeine hits from your local Starbucks to get you through a busy morning. 'Crash and burn' is all that will happen. The best breakfasts are protein-based, and my favourite is eggs. Protein will keep you fuller for longer, sustain your energy levels for longer and satisfy your appetite. Eggs don't take a huge amount of time to cook. Have them scrambled, poached or boiled, but without bread!! If you still love your porridge, then that's no problem. Just make sure you add nuts and seeds.

I don't expect you to be good 100% of the time, after all we are only human, but I do expect you to be consistent eight out of ten times. If you try too hard to be 100% perfect with your diet all the time, you will fail and no one likes to fail. So get some balance and give yourself some room.

Have a 'cheat day' occasionally because you deserve it. If you achieve a goal, your reward to yourself could be to eat that big cream cake or bar of chocolate. We are still human after all and I don't think it's unreasonable to have a treat so don't feel guilty or negative if you do so. But we must still be accountable and responsible for what we eat. As you know, eating too much of the wrong type of food is bad for both body and mind. Allowing yourself an occasional 'cheat day' lets you look forward to having those 'treat' foods without feeling guilty about them. There is no need to be too extreme; it will only screw up your results!

Which brings me to my next subject - especially designed for weight-conscious executives!! Yes, if you know that you need to lose weight, you're right that you need to cut down on the amount of food you're putting into your body. If you take my advice on board, then you will not only become healthier, but you will also lose weight naturally. My advice is not to become addicted to the scales. When you weigh yourself, the scales don't take your muscle and water content into consideration. Measure your energy levels and waist-size, if you want to measure your progress.

One of the questions my clients most frequently ask is, "What if I have to work during my lunch hour?". I really do understand that when you're busy at work - running a team, networking with potential clients, securing deals, or meeting deadlines, etc. – then lunch-time eating can often be forgotten. But your health is just as important as your work – probably more so!! So if you're saying lunch is 'impossible', think about what you are saying. If you commit to making time for a healthy lunch-time snack with the same passion and dedication you give to your work and career, then I believe you can make it happen. Improving your lifestyle is not only going to benefit you in the long term, but also offset some of your unwanted stress, especially from the effects of alcohol and rich restaurant foods.

So let me help you... Eat a handful of nuts and lean meats before heading out.

1. Avoid buffet style or 'eat-all-you-can' restaurants

2. Don't go out on an empty stomach

3. Go for the salad bar minus the fatty dressings. (Note that balsamic vinegar, French dressing and olive oil are fine).

4. Stay away from the dreaded bread basket!!

5. Go for items on the menu that have been prepared healthily, such as boiled, steamed and roasted vegetables

6. Keep low GI in mind and order the most suitable choice available

7. Limit your intake of alcoholic beverages

10 nutrition challenges

1. Never skip breakfast

2. Eat three main meals and two snacks daily

3. Drink a 1.5 litre bottle of water daily. Your body is made of around 70% water so it's obvious how important keeping it hydrated is for survival. Poor concentration levels and poor training can lead you to feeling tired and thirsty. If you are thirsty as you read this book you are already dehydrated! Drink water regularly throughout the day.

4. Eat protein with every meal

5. Stay away from bread, potatoes and pasta

6. Avoid breakfast cereal. Most breakfast cereals contain more sugar than a can of Coke. I call cereal the 'devil's food'!!

7. Avoid fried fatty foods as most are cooked in trans-fatty acids. Most of these foods have a high calorie content and low nutrient content.

8. Stay away from the microwave. Microwave meals generally consist of highly processed foods which contain excess amounts of sodium, increasing your blood pressure and increasing your risks of coronary heart disease.

9. Cook 'fresh' at every occasion. Preparing food is a learning experience. It will also take you on an educational journey to learn what's good for you and what foods make you healthy.

10. Avoid fruit juices. Many people think that fruit juices are healthy and contribute towards our 'five-a-day'. But they're wrong. Most juices, especially those from concentrate, contain more sugar than a can of fizzy drink. Excess sugar in your diet means excess fat.

The five nutrition challenges while you're away from home.

1. Find out in advance about the foods that the hotel you're staying in typically serves.

2. Locate the nearest shop or supermarket where you can buy organic or wholefoods and fresh produce (whole foods are generally a good choice).

3. Use only bottled water or filtered water which is much healthier than tap water. (Also, if abroad, you need to ensure any non-bottled water is safe to drink).

4. Locate markets with fresh produce.

5. Check cooked or fresh food before consuming it. If it doesn't look good or it's lukewarm in temperature don't touch it and send it back!

Here are some quick, nutritious meals that take just 10 to 15 minutes to prepare. So you can easily incorporate them into your routine:

1. Vegetable omelette – 2or 3 eggs (organic or free-range) with chopped vegetables of your own choice.

2. Grilled haddock with mixed vegetables and sweet potatoes.

3. Tuna jacket sweet potato - bake a sweet potato and fill with fresh or tinned tuna, low fat mayo, sweet corn and steamed broccoli.

4. Baked salmon with almonds, served with asparagus, broccoli, sweet corn and sweet potato.

5. Shish kebab – place lean steak, turkey or chicken on a skewer with peppers, onions and mushrooms. Then grill. Serve with vegetables.

6. 'Chef's salad' - lean turkey, ham or chicken with a sliced hard-boiled egg, teaspoon of low-fat cheese, mixed vegetables, lettuce, tomatoes, guacamole and fat-free dressing.

Chapter 9: Tips for team-goal achievement

The first part of developing your business into a gold-medal worthy enterprise is to establish your own goals and those of your team members. To have a goal, you simply need to have purpose, focus and motivation in achieving that objective. In this chapter, I'm going to show you a simple way to set your team's goals, how your employees can set personal goals and a simple formula to achieve them. But before we do that, I'm going to give you some very simple guidelines on how to write your goals.

> *"Goals are the fuel in the furnace of achievement"*
>
> *Brian Tracy*

1. Don't just think about your goals, write them down. Writing down your goals is key as otherwise they may get 'lost in translation' as new issues and situations arise in your life. So don't get distracted: write each goal down straight away.

2. Suspend reality. Take a step out and detach yourself from the current reality of your world. Right now, if you had every resource, ability and skill imaginable, what would you do with these assets? How could you make your life better than it is today? What could you accomplish and whom could you influence? Don't hold back: don't allow your current abilities and skills to limit you. Allow your thoughts and imagination to transcend reality! At this point, you should be simply brainstorming ideas. You don't need to start committing to anything or writing down goals. Have you ever read or watched 'Aladdin'? The genie has the power to grant three wishes. Well, I'm going to let you have ten! So go for it and write down your ten wishes.

3. Give yourself permission to think and dream as big as you want. If you could guarantee success at the end of the journey, what would you go for? What your big ambition in life or what have you always wanted to do? What is the one outrageous goal that makes your palms sweat and increases your heart rate? What gives you that surge of adrenalin?

> *"We all have dreams. But in order to make dreams come into reality, it takes an awful lot of determination, dedication, self-discipline, and effort"*
>
> *Jesse Owens*

4. Stay positively focused by deciding what you want in order to move towards it, not away from it. I find visualisation helps me with this exercise. Examples of positive visualisation could include, "My company will be recognised as one of the fastest growing companies in Fortune 500 magazine by December 2020" or "I will be featured as a keynote speaker at X conference by the summer of 2018".

5. Visualise yourself as how you want to be by saying, "I am" in contrast to "I want to be". This will help you switch on the creative side of your brain since you have now declared how you see yourself. Doing this empowers you to become whom you say you are.

6. Be sure to really own your goals:

A goal is just a wish unless it is written down.

What is the goal?
Use smart

Barriers
Negatives
Anxiety
Not achievable
Phobias
I can't do attitude

Solutions
Positives
Bite size goals
Positive thinking

Strategy

Goal Achieved

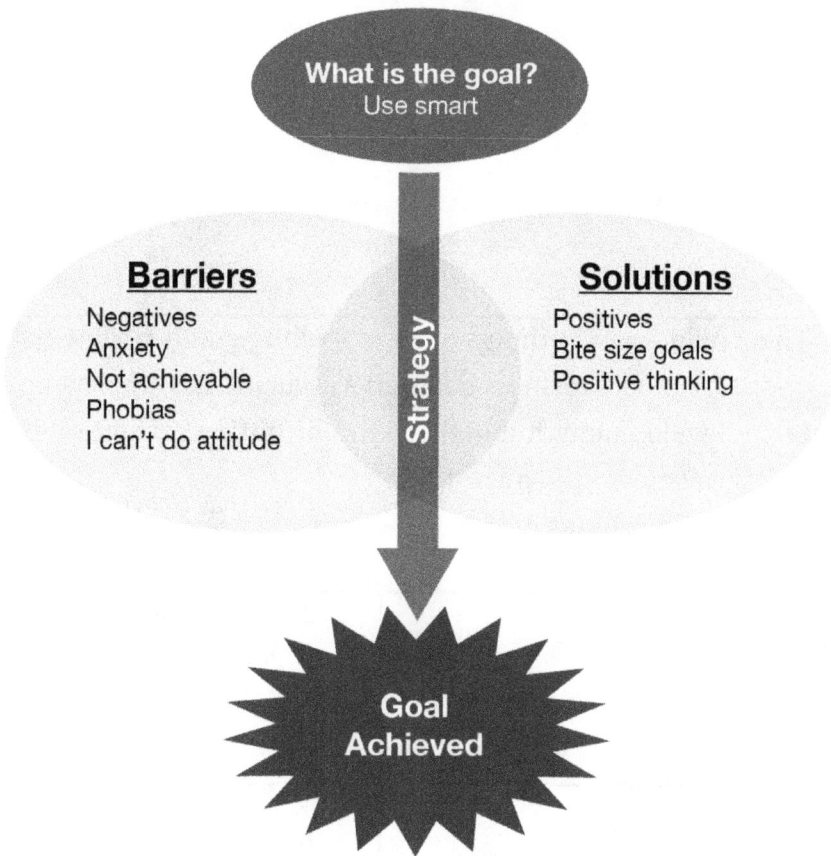

Many people set goals because they feel they are the types of goal they ought to aspire to rather than the ones they really want for themselves. Don't let friends, family, work peers or social pressures dictate to you what your dreams and desires should be. You and your team's goals need to come from your hearts and inner selves. By not setting yourself goals that are truly your own, you will not really believe you are capable of achieving them and, as a result, you will most likely fail to meet them because they are something that you didn't really want anyway.

Now I want you to write down and list your goals for each of the eight priority areas of your life. You are not being held accountable at this point. We will come to that later. Whatever comes into your mind, write it down. You don't necessarily have to fill in all eight priority areas, but try to fill in as many as you can.

Business

This could include things such as planning and reviewing your career and business goals on a regular basis, improving team development, finding a coach, or hitting certain sales targets, achieving an award, etc.	
1.	2.
3.	4.
5.	6.
7.	8.

Financial

These could include beginning an investment plan, paying off your credit cards, setting up a savings account, reducing your company debt, saving for your children's university fees, setting up a private pension, or giving to charity, etc.	
1.	2.
3.	4.
5.	6.
7.	8.

Physical

This could include running a marathon, improving your posture, reducing your blood pressure, completing 10,000 steps on a pedometer, reducing the amount of fried, fatty food in your diet, reducing alcohol consumption, cutting down on caffeine, or working with a corporate health consultancy, etc.

1.	2.
3.	4.
5.	6.
7.	8.

Mental

This could include reading personal development and growth books, undertaking positive visualisation, managing your time more effectively, developing a team vision board, etc.	
1.	2.
3.	4.
5.	6.
7.	8.

Family

This might include spending more time with your family, making sure you are home on time for dinner with the family, planning outings, reading bedtime stories to your children, organising an evening out for you and your partner, etc.

1.	2.
3.	4.
5.	6.
7.	8.

Spiritual

This might include organising a mindfulness session, taking up yoga, or exploring spiritual or religious beliefs, etc.

1.	2.
3.	4.
5.	6.
7.	8.

Lifestyle

This might include travelling to new holiday destinations, exploring new places where you might like to live, identifying new people you would like to meet, spending time on your hobbies, learning a foreign language, taking part in adventure activities, learning a musical instrument, cutting back on business travel, etc.

1.	2.
3.	4.
5.	6.
7.	8.

Relationships

This might include remembering to send birthday cards to family and team members, stopping or limiting contact with negative people, spending more time with close friends, planning breaks away with a partner, identifying relationships you would like to develop, etc.

1.	2.
3.	4.
5.	6.
7.	8.

Top ten: Now we need to sort out and prioritise your top ten goals from the list above. Use this checklist to define your top ten goals. This will help you narrow them down from the lists above. Put a letter against each category, e.g. R = relationship, then your goal, the date by which you are going to reach the goal, and the risks and rewards in achieving the goal.

Your top ten goals

Category	Goal	Deadline	Risk	Reward

Category	Goal	Deadline	Risk	Reward

> *"Without goals and plans to reach them, you are like a ship that has set sail with no destination"*
>
> **Fitzhugh Dodson**

Setting goals the 'smart way'

I'm sure you have seen this before, but I think this is a very simple way of constructing goals. I'm sure you're probably already very familiar with using the S.M.A.R.T. method when setting business goals or working with your team.

S = Specific: this means the goal is clear, defined and recognisable to anyone.

An example could be, "I want to increase sales by 10% in the next three months" versus "I want more sales".

M = Measurable: measuring your progress is very important and motivating as it helps you stay on track, reach your target dates and experience the importance of accomplishing goals at each individual step ('little wins'). Measurement helps drive you on to continuing your efforts and achieving your goals. In order to measure a particular goal, ask yourself questions, such as, "How will I know when I've achieved this goal?".

An example of a measurable goal is "I need to invest X amount over the next three months in order to achieve a sales increase of 10%" versus simply saying "I want more revenue".

A = Attainable or Achievable. Try not to live up in the clouds with your goals. For example, you're not going to solve the problem of world hunger by the end of the month or lose half your body weight by the end of next week. Don't just rely on sheer luck to achieve your goal. It won't happen without your commitment and effort.

R = Relevant. Make sure that your goals relate to the core beliefs you wrote down earlier. Your goals must be aligned to the vision you have of your life and what you want to get out of it.

T = Timely. I'm sure that every day and week you have deadlines that you need to meet. Achieving your goals should be realistic, but also an exciting challenge. You need to be in a position to step up to the challenge. Leaders like you excel at challenges. While you need sufficient time to achieve the goals that you and your team have set yourselves, you should be hungry to accomplish them.

Now finally, you need to make sure your goals are 'balanced'. You and your team should review your 10 individual goals and make sure that they represent each area of the 'Circle of Success'. The overall goal is to achieve success in every area of your life. Don't end up as the person with a 20-room mansion in the country, but no family to share it with, or the guy in the gym with big, muscular arms, but with weak, skinny legs.

What you get by achieving your goals is not as important as what you become by achieving your goals

Zig Ziglar

Chapter 10: Investing in yourself and your team

> *"There is no magic formula for great company culture. The key is just to treat your staff how you would like to be treated"*
>
> *Richard Branson*

C elebrate! Yes, you have achieved it - you have fulfilled your destiny. If you haven't completed the tasks and activities in the book, then go back right now! I didn't write this book for my benefit, I did it for you and your business. So before you read on, complete the tasks to the best of your ability.

Before I show you how to invest in yourself and your workforce, you need to know why investment is important.

Your journey through this book should have taught you valuable lessons, and one of those lessons is to begin to value your life and those around you. Be thankful for your support networks, friends, work colleagues and family members, and even me! You also should now have a re-focused purpose in life: able to compare and contrast your life now to how it was before. Your goal in life is not just to work, work, work. It's about establishing a sensible work/life balance through achieving a positive mindset and using fitness, nutritional and lifestyle strategies that work for you.

On that note, it's important to invest, not just in yourself, but also in your team!! You will find that the lifestyle you create will have an impact on your team in particular. Your life will become fulfilled and you and your business will be able to thrive, not just survive. If you want to get more out of your life, then it's important to think of others before yourself. The only person that puts unnecessary stress into your life is you! With the clients I've worked with, I've found that in 95% of cases arguments with their loved ones are the result of long hours at work. If you believe you need to work more hours to get away from arguments and nagging, it's because of your own insecurity. You're simply satisfying your ego. Your priority should be to put your team's needs first. We all have choices in life. Whether you make the right choice is down to you!

As a decision-maker, you have the power to share your positive experiences in order to create a vibrant work culture. Your team will begin to evolve and send out the clear message that "If you want more out of life, then live it". Your team will become more productive. They will become more creative thinkers and more motivated. And it will all be because of you! Your positive, vibrant work ethic will not just make your team members happy, it will also allow them to deliver better results whilst reducing unnecessary pressures on them.

As people around you start to notice the positive change in you, your business will reap the benefits and your team will start to grow. As you become more motivated, your enthusiasm increases; you smile more and generally look more relaxed and happy. You're able to focus on working on the business not in the business as your team starts to take ownership.

Let's quickly backtrack to where I talked about 'the self'. I want you to go back to when you started on this journey. I spoke about your 'present self' and your 'ideal self'. What was that image that you had locked up in your mind? What were the characteristics, personality and attitudes you attributed to your ideal self? Now the big question is do you feel like you're now more aligned to your ideal self? Or does it feel like you've still got a long way to go? If the answer is you still feel miles away, then did you complete the tasks fully as set out for you and have you been honest with yourself? Go back, if you haven't completed the activities set out and dedicate some time for yourself. If you have completed the tasks and you and others do see the change, then great! I congratulate you!

Staying aligned with your ideal self is very important because it means you're able to stay on track and keep motivated. You can do this by reviewing your goals and setting new challenges. In order to stay motivated, you should look for innovative and creative ways to keep yourself interested. As you adapt, you must consistently look for the next big thing, whatever it may be.

To start investing in yourself, I recommend making a list of hobbies and interests that you would like to do more of and put a date in your diary by when you are going to start doing them. It could be playing with model trains, going out cycling, fishing, salsa classes, cooking or playing cricket, etc. But make sure you give yourself sufficient space to do your chosen activities at least three times a week. I would also recommend you make up a 'bucket list' of all the things you want to do. It could be to train as a scuba diver; it could be to write a book; or see the Seven Wonders of the World, etc., etc. Whatever it may be, get it in that bucket! The next thing to do is to prioritise what you're going to do first and by when you're going to do it. Some things in your bucket list might not happen for ten years but it will definitely give you something to look forward to!

My programmes aren't for the faint hearted but, if you and your team want ultimately to achieve your business and personal goals, you will begin to see changes not just in your mind but also in your body. Most of my clients normally need to recruit more people, move to bigger offices or expand into new markets. Your business is going to be transformed! You're going to stop feeling frustrated and you and your team will feel happier, healthier and more engaged.

My life is fulfilled

> *"Purpose is what gives life a meaning."*
>
> *C. H. Parkhurst*

In order to fulfill your change commitments, you and your team simply need to stay in that positive mindset and consistently work on learning and growing.

As I mentioned before with regards to Adam's hierarchy of human needs, let me ask you a question, "Are you on the road to achieving self-actualisation?". Most people don't ever achieve self-actualisation, purely because they don't believe in themselves. However, you should work your hardest to push forwards towards that goal. Nelson Mandela is known for tackling apartheid, poverty and inequality in South Africa. Mother Teresa is known for setting up orphanages for homeless children, providing hospices for people with HIV/AIDS, and helping the poorest of the poor. These are extreme cases, but you too can make an impact by helping others. I recently completed one of the hardest off-road cycle races in the UK in order to raise money for a local children's hospice.

One of the ways I get my clients to focus is to visualise. This is a very powerful tool. Close your eyes and create a thought in your head. What do you see? Do you see your company being recognised as one of the best companies to work? Do you see yourself sprinting across the finish line in a marathon? Powerful, isn't it? How does it make you feel? What do you need to do? I recommend you visualise at least twice a day for at least 10 minutes each time. Use this time to really feel, touch and become part of that experience.

Get yourself booked into Bikram Yoga. Bikram yoga is series of yoga postures and breathing techniques performed in a heated room. The yoga posture sequences will help maximise oxygenation and detoxification of the entire body. It is a fantastic way to develop strength and flexibility and to counter a sedentary lifestyle. It brings with it body vitality, health and a sense of complete well-being. The heat will help facilitate stretching and prevention of injuries, while the sweating will be very useful in helping the body remove waste products.

You can also develop positive thinking by simply changing your environment more often. Changing your environment is stimulating to the body and mind. The change could be a walk in the country, enjoying the sights of the beach, or listening to calming music (which can be very helpful in winding down after a busy day).

By being more positive you are simply building your self-confidence. There are a number of ways to achieve this. One approach is to go out and do more networking and strengthen your relationships with clients by finding more ways to create a 'WOW' service for them. Another approach is to give someone in your team responsibility for organising social events. This will help promote a positive mindset and create team spirit. Thirdly, take regular breaks. These will allow you to reflect on how your day has gone, what you have achieved, and on better ways to do things.

One of the things that truly relaxes me is imagining myself sitting on a sandy beach. I close my eyes and just listen to the waves! The energy from my imagined waves gives me a sense of peace and tranquillity. Meditation is proven to help the rest mind and relax you so try doing it for 15 to 20 minutes every day.

There are many different ways to meditate and I would recommend you explore which one works for you. The simplest way is to simply stop what you are doing right now!! Just take a second and breathe, switch off, and empty all your thoughts. The only thing that you need to concentrate on is inhaling and exhaling. What do you feel?

You don't need to be locked away from civilisation to enjoy meditation. Enjoy the moment you are living in. Don't be weighed down by other people or your schedule. Just taking that moment in your life will give you far greater benefits in return. Regular practice of 'being in the moment' will enable you to experience a greater sense of clarity, balance, positivity and energy which you can take with you for the rest of your day.

Now it's all about maintenance and keeping up your hard work.

Tip: Keep a journal and write it up daily. Write down what you have done today, what challenges you have encountered, how you overcame them and what your achievements were.

Set yourself weekly goals that maintain your focus and drive. Inspirational leaders are not born, they are made. What is it you wish to achieve? What are your lifetime ambitions?

When setting a goal, dream 'big' and you will believe in it.

Story: Michael Phelps is one of the greatest Olympians who ever lived. Phelps speaks very much about the origins of his success and how from an early age setting goals in his life became vitally important. He received this advice from his two older sisters and from the age of seven started to regularly set goals. At the age of 11, his coach told him if he worked hard enough he would be good enough to compete in the next Olympics in Sydney in 2000. So he got to work and became the youngest American swimmer in 68 years to compete in the Olympics. In 2001 at the age of 15, he then went on to break the world record in the 200-metre butterfly. But that simply was not enough. In the 2004 Olympic Games in Athens, he won six gold medals but wanted to push the bar even higher. Competing in the Beijing Olympics in 2008, he had already earned six gold medals, but then, with two more races to run, he began to feel tired and de-motivated. He said

You can't put a
limit on anything.
The more you dream,
the farther you get.

Michael Phelps

to his coach, "I have nothing left. I'm drained". With the help of his coach and through his own determination, he managed to finish the last two races purely on sheer adrenalin bringing his total of gold medals in Beijing to eight. In addition, he broke the world record in every event he competed in except one. His quote is:

> *"Dream big and never give up ."*
>
> *Michael Phelps*

Set up a personal development corner in your office so you and your team can access motivational materials. These resources will help you and your team grow, develop new skills and learn from inspirational thinkers, giving you the opportunity to enhance everyone's creative thinking abilities and build new business opportunities.

How do you view your life? Is it fulfilled yet? If you haven't quite got there yet, don't worry. The most important thing is working on getting there. It's not a race. You're not in competition with anyone else. It's just you. Having a fulfilled life should mean happiness. How do you view happiness? What does it look like?

Happiness is personal to each of us, but it does share universal characteristics. Happiness is about living in harmony. This means the more you understand and are at ease with who you are and your abilities, the more likely you are to understand and appreciate the rest of humanity. Harmony is a feeling that you are happy, content and that your mind and emotions are well balanced. Happiness is about valuing your treasured moments, time with friends and family and never taking life for granted. You never know what's around the corner! Someone who is truly fulfilled detaches themselves from the ego, recognising that by just existing they are touching the lives of others. My recommendation is do something for other people. In the past, I have helped raise thousands of pounds for children's charities by participating in regular running events. I have also helped run and support community groups that encourage young people to participate in sports.

Do something for charity, whether that is volunteering to work on health programmes in Africa or running in the London Marathon for a cancer charity. Doing something like this will put you up on that journey of self-actualisation.

Giving something back could involve you being part of a community group, such as the scouts or guides, a business start-up community group or a networking business event.

Having a fulfilled life means also needing and wanting success. What do you want to be successful at? What do you want to be known for? What do you want to expand your knowledge in?

You can be successful at anything you want to be. When I mention the words 'success' or 'successful people', what comes to mind? Being successful is having the feeling of a sense of accomplishment. You have conquered and mastered your ambitions and you have found solutions that work for you. Who would you like to dedicate your success to? Some of the great success stories that come to mind reflect the skills covered in this book. It's all about believing in yourself and having commitment.

> *"Success is knowing your purpose in life,*
> *growing to reach your maximum potential,*
> *and sowing seeds that benefit others."*
>
> *John Maxwell*

Walt Disney was fired from a newspaper because they say he lacked imagination and had no good ideas. He is an international icon and the Disney Corporation is now worth $36 billion.

When Thomas Edison was young, his teacher told him that he was too stupid to learn anything. Yet after perseverance and failing over a thousand times, he invented the light bulb.

J.K. Rowling has gone from 'rags to riches'. Her first husband left her and she had to bring up two young daughters by herself. Now as a result of the famous 'Harry Potter' novels, she is one of the most successful authors of all time.

The point I'm making is that you don't have to be a superstar to succeed. Whenever someone says, "You're not talented enough", "You're not good enough" or "You can't achieve that", simply don't accept it!! Believe in yourself and ignore such distractions. You will put yourself on track for achieving total well-being.

My 'STRONG' programme is designed to help successful business leaders work smarter, not harder. I can empower you and your team to make the right choices, re-energise the body, mind and spirit, and transform you and your team into champions by enhancing performance and productivity.

It's time for action

This is the end of my book and, in celebration, I'm going to see the big screening of 'Willy Wonka' at the Drury Lane Theatre in London with my son. Now you can do one of two things with this book: either place it on a bookshelf to gather dust and continue with your busy, stressed life; or you can use it to create a new beginning - a whole new way to live your life. How many books have you read on fitness, nutrition or health? Don't use this book just to accompany some new 'fad' diet. You will get discouraged and it will be something you will want to forget.

It's time for **implementation** and this is where the fun part starts. I want you to succeed and I'm confident you can. It's up to you. Taking control of your health should be your number one priority, especially if you want to be a business leader. Your health will reflect what happens in the workplace and your success as a leader.

This book sets out a path. But you have to choose which path you will take. So choose the path that gives you joy in abundance. Remember to have a plan that is simple, easy-to-follow and enjoyable. Don't forget to enjoy your life. Book that holiday, attend that sports day or do something stupendous, such as when I hiked across the Grand Canyon!

Take control of your health before it's too late and see a professional to discuss your health and fitness plan. Focus on the three main aspects of wellbeing: psychological (mindset), nutrition (energy) and physiological (body and stress management). You will notice in a short period of time that you will begin to sleep better, have more energy, be more productive and focused. Make lifestyle changes and celebrate them. Turn off all work communication after 7pm. Use a Swiss ball instead of a chair at your desk. Commit to getting fresh air for at least 60 minutes every day. These are big things - so don't overlook them.

By now, you should have a better understanding of how health and stress management go hand-in-hand, and what can go wrong if you don't do something about them. You understand that your thoughts about work/life balance can change your mindset, energy levels and motivation. You are ready to ask for expert help and, by using one of our programmes, we can help you achieve a de-stressed life and a re-energised body and mind. If you just have a small belief, then hold on to it and build on it! I believe that every business leader can achieve a good work /life balance and feel de-stressed and inspired. You will see a transformation like no other. You'll feel and look great, and others around you will notice, too. You will be oozing self-confidence and positive ego, and have a profound positive impact on others, leaving you feeling so much younger. Now that's something worth celebrating!

For those of you who want ongoing support, or to share challenges, stories, frustrations and celebrations, you can join others on our social media sites devoted to this book.

*A real decision
is measured
by the fact that
you've taken a
new action.
If there's no action,
you haven't
truly decided.*

Tony Robbins

Step up and move to the next level!

As with the many things in life, reading a book is one thing, implementing what you have learned is another.

As a thank you for purchasing and reading this book, I'd like to offer you something of real value. I'd like to make a free initial projection of how much money I can save your business.

To benefit from this free initial projection, all you have to do is contact me at hello@adamstrong.net to arrange a time to suit you. My aim is to help you achieve a return on investment of up to 300% in relation to your higher paid staff.

I also offer 'lunch and learn' sessions and one-day workshops (see the back of this book).

I look forward to working with you!

www.elitecorporatefitness.com/blog/

www.adamstrong.net

www.twitter.com/adamistrong

www.linkedin.com/in/adamistrong

If you would like to review this book, we will reward you for taking your time for doing so. Here's how:

1. Write a review of this book

2. Post it on the following: Amazon, iTunes bookstore, your Facebook page or your blog

3. Send the link or a screenshot to the following email address: hello@adamstrong.net

4. One of the team will contact you or your company to arrange a free 45-minute 'lunch and learn' session (valued at £625), subject to your location. You can also receive samples of new products/services from Elite Corporate Fitness.

Bibliography

Why Should We Get Eight Hours Sleep? BBC News. http://news.bbc.co.uk. April 12 2007. 'Accessed July 29th 2013

Back Pain (nd) available online: http://www.enetmd.com/content/back-pain. Accessed July 29th 2013

CERIELLO A and MOTZ E (2004) *Is Oxidative Stress The Pathogenic Mechanism Underlying Insulin Resistance, Diabetes And Cardiovascular Disease?* Arteriosclerosis, Thrombosis and Vascular biology. 24, 816-823

CHAPMAN L (2012) Stress in the City. *Therapy Today.* Vol 23, Issue 1

COHEN JS (2001) *Overdose: The Case Against The Drug Companies.* 1st Edition, New York, New York: Penguin Putman

FOX M (2010) *U.S Dietary Supplements Often Contaminated Report.* Available online: http://www.reuters.com/article/2010/08/03/us-usa-supplements-idUSTRE6721F520100803

VAN GAAL L, MERTENS I and DE BLOCK C (2006) Mechanisms Linking Obesity With Cardiovascular Disease. *Nature.* 444, 875-880

WHIPPLE T (2011) *Banks Keep Shtoom About Stress In The City.* The Times. http://www.thetimes.co.uk/tto/life/article3219288.ece

*Exercise is the catalyst.
That's what makes everything
happen: your digestion, your
elimination, your sex life, your
skin, hair, everything about you
depends on circulation.
And how do you
increase circulation?*

Jack LaLanne

www.ingramcontent.com/pod-product-compliance
Lightning Source LLC
Chambersburg PA
CBHW050724030426
42336CB00012B/1411